Praise for

BORN TO EAT

"*Born to Eat* answered all my questions about baby-led weaning. Leslie and Wendy Jo will help parents raise children who feel good about food and their bodies, which is preventative medicine at its best. I wish this book had been around when my daughter was a baby! Highly recommended for new parents."
—Katja Rowell, MD, author of *Helping Your Child with Extreme Picky Eating*

"What comes over in this easy-to-read book is that moving on to solid foods should be a positive experience, and that we can trust our babies to know their own bodies. By choosing healthy foods and being present and purposeful at shared family mealtimes, we can feel confident to sit back and let our children make their own discoveries and decisions—because we are all *Born to Eat.*"
—Gill Rapley, PhD, coauthor of *Baby-Led Weaning*

"*Born to Eat* emphasizes two of the most important aspects of child feeding that also happen to be lacking in our society today: connection and trust. Leslie and Wendy Jo combine their professional experience with their parenting wisdom to remind us that feeding our children is supposed to be a simple, fun, and nurturing experience, rather than one of stress, guilt, and worry. *Born to Eat* protects a child's ability to self-regulate their intake and nurtures their innate curiosity of food. For any parents considering the baby-led weaning approach or an approach that fosters a healthy relationship with food for the entire family, *Born to Eat* is a must!"
—Lindsay Stenovec, MS, RD, CEDRD, owner of Nutrition Instincts & founder of The Nurtured Mama Club

"Problem solved! *Born to Eat* is like a trustworthy friend showing you the ropes of feeding your infant with love and compassion. As new parents, we care deeply about doing what's best for baby, but food can be especially overwhelming. Read this book and experience the joys of watching your child explore eating with curiosity and engagement. Leslie and Wendy Jo give you the information you need and the permission to make it work for your family through the years."
—Rebecca Scritchfield, author of *Body Kindness*

"*Born To Eat* is a must-read for anyone thinking about trying baby-led weaning. It's a practical guide that provides simple, actionable steps for each stage of the process and addresses all of the common questions and fears that many parents have."
—Lindsay Livingston, RD, founder of *The Lean Green Bean* blog

BORN TO EAT

BORN TO EAT

WHOLE, HEALTHY FOODS
FROM BABY'S FIRST BITE

LESLIE SCHILLING, MA, RDN & WENDY JO PETERSON, MS, RDN

Skyhorse Publishing

Disclaimer

This book contains suggestions and advice for starting solid foods with your infant. It is not a substitute for medical care or medical advice. All infants and families are different, so please discuss this process with your pediatrician and other members of your support team.

Skyhorse Publishing books may be purchased in bulk at special discounts for sales promotion, corporate gifts, fund-raising, or educational purposes. Special editions can also be created to specifications. For details, contact the Special Sales Department, Skyhorse Publishing, 307 West 36th Street, 11th Floor, New York, NY 10018 or info@skyhorsepublishing.com.

Skyhorse® and Skyhorse Publishing® are registered trademarks of Skyhorse Publishing, Inc.®, a Delaware corporation.

Visit our website at www.skyhorsepublishing.com.

10 9 8 7 6 5 4

Library of Congress Cataloging-in-Publication Data is available on file.

Cover design: Jenny Zemanek

Cover photo credit: iStock

Print ISBN: 978-1-5107-1999-6

Ebook ISBN: 978-1-5107-2001-5

Printed in China

To CC and Anya:

Because of you, we've embraced our own good-enoughness knowing that is the surest way for you to claim your own. Never forget that you are fearfully and wonderfully made, our loves. You two brought *Born to Eat* to life, and we pray that you will confidently enjoy each bite this life has to offer.

And

To B and B:

You're the most supportive and loving copilots two rule-breaker women could ever ask for. Thank you for not only trusting us on this journey with your favorite baby girls, but also showing the world there are *Born to Eat* dads, too.

CONTENTS

INTRODUCTION

The simple act of eating has become so overly complicated. It can be nerve-racking simply to attempt to feed ourselves well, much less our children. It doesn't have to be that way.

Parents are some of the most talented, selfless, and overwhelmed people out there. We're parents; we know! What mom, dad, or caregiver wouldn't want to reduce anxiety around feeding and increase our confidence in nourishing our kids? As nutrition experts (and moms) who've worked in the dietetics field from pediatrics to pro sports, we're cutting through the hype and fads to make feeding better for baby and, hopefully, less stressful for mom and dad. We believe that infants (and adults) are *Born to Eat*.

Born to Eat is a philosophy that we feel supports a lifelong, healthy relationship with food and body that begins with a self-feeding approach as an infant. This is the process that we use with our own kids not just because it makes sense and has been around since the dawn of man, but because it has a growing body of research to support it, as well. Infants supported in this approach are eating healthy foods and becoming natural eaters most likely with incredible feeding confidence and self-regulation skills. We believe that self-feeding whole foods is a successful method. Our entire population wouldn't exist if it wasn't.

In our society, people are constantly bombarded with confusing and conflicting messages from social media, the Internet, well-meaning friends, or even health professionals. We, Wendy Jo and Leslie, have taken the research and coupled it with our professional and personal experiences to start clearing up the nutritional mumbo-jumbo that can make us overthink food, feeding, and trusting our bodies for a lifetime. This is one of the main reasons we decided to write *Born to Eat*. That, and the fact that we are *Born to Eat*.

Our Journeys to Self-Feeding

Leslie's daughter was five days old when friends came to visit. They didn't come empty-handed, either—they came with food, really good food, and the book *Baby-Led Weaning* by Gill Rapley and Tracey Murkett. They spoke of how they were using baby-led weaning with their son, and right away Leslie was interested—partly because the thought of making baby food was absolutely daunting and partly because eating real food (as much as possible but don't get crazy) was her motto. Being the geeks Leslie and her husband are, they studied the emerging research on baby-led weaning and interviewed experienced professionals before starting their daughter, CC, with her first piece of steak, egg, avocado, etc. It just made sense: no pricey pastel blenders or purées in ice cube trays while baby learns about taste, texture, and develops fine motor skills by eating whole foods . . . Where do we sign up?

It's not easy; learning a new skill never is. Leslie's family is one that likes to cook most meals and sit down to eat together. This was a very helpful habit already in place. Regardless, it takes time and it's messy, but oh so worth it. Today, Leslie's daughter will eat a brownie or donut and—get ready—leave some on her plate. They have no doubt that allowing her to develop her innate feeding skills and body trust through a self-feeding approach played a very important role in that.

Leslie and her husband were so grateful their friends brought them that book; it ignited a spark in Leslie because she knew it wasn't just about the food, but about the family attitude and behaviors around food that can shape a child for lifetime. And that shaping happens mostly at home in the family environment very early in life. Leslie has spent more than fifteen years working with children and adults who never got to develop (or have lost) their own body trust. We feel that this approach can help change that. It starts with self-feeding, but the *Born to Eat* approach is so much more.

After watching Leslie embark on this journey with CC, and our dietitian colleague and friend, Rebecca Scritchfield, with her two little ones, Wendy Jo was convinced this journey was for her. Like many parents, she was eager to get started, chomping at the bit for all the signs of readiness. When her daughter turned five and a half months old, they began the journey of self-feeding whole foods. Without giving too much away just yet, Wendy Jo shares that this has been the most rewarding part of parenthood for her family. As a nutrition professional, food ranks pretty high up there in her household, and they look forward to mealtimes as a family. Now Wendy Jo's daughter, Miss A, shares in the joys of eating with the family; whether dinner is Thai, Indian, Mexican, or Italian (her favorite) food, she's all in. With this approach, parents can become far more relaxed and baby can take the lead with self-feeding. It was apparent to Wendy Jo and her husband that Miss A was also *Born to Eat*.

Perfectly Imperfect

First off, let's get something straight: this isn't a perfect parenting book. Nor is this book a perfect nutrition book. We are not perfect parents, and even though we are nutrition experts, we don't eat perfectly. Like you, we're parents doing the best we can. What we do promise is to share the best information we have (thankfully not always conventional), comforting steps, nutrition tips, stories, and our own journeys. We want your family to feel great about the family plate without overthinking food. Join us as we walk the perfectly imperfect path to parenthood while living in a very nutritionally confusing world. We'll start with our no-nonsense guide to self-feeding beginning at about six months of age, then we'll carry you through the late infant and toddler stages. We'll take the tenets of baby-led weaning and self-feeding and guide you through feeding your little one. Our hope is that this process will not only be a liberating experience for you and your family, but will also help you promote body confidence in your child (and hopefully yourself). You might just get more meals seated at the family table while you're at it. It won't be perfect, but it will be real.

It's hard out there as a parent. We live in a culture of misinformation and shaming; food shaming, body shaming, parent shaming, you name it! If it's not *eat this to be healthy*, it's *here's the path to a perfect body* (which is only an illusion of photo editing). We even hear things like *if you're not eating this* (insert fad of the week) *or doing this diet, you should be ashamed*. Let's face it, we live in a culture that thinks shaming is a sport (it's sad and sick). If you're not doing what others are doing, then you're wrong, a hippie, lazy, or just crazy. We absolutely do not want shaming of any kind to be a part of the *Born to Eat* philosophy or community. For this reason, we feel it's important for us to share *our* definitions of certain words and phrases with you here and throughout the book. We just want you to know where we're coming from when we use one of these terms. And no matter what, don't forget this phrase: *what you chew is up to you!*

Born To Eat Basic Terminology

Processed food—Unless you picked it right off the vine, it's processed in some way to get to you. If you pick up an apple in the grocery, it's been processed, meaning someone picked it and got it to the store. Frozen berries are processed to get in that bag and in the freezer bin. The sirloin steak was processed and placed in the meat section yet still has one ingredient: beef. Processed foods are normal, we all use them, and many are considered whole foods.

Overly processed food—In our opinion, overly processed foods aren't even close to their normal or natural state. They have been refined, heavily altered, and/or chemically processed. This may be a food (or food-like item) made with refined flours, artificial sweeteners, artificial colors, artificial flavors, added fillers, with the normally occurring fats removed, and so on. Our least favorite of these are the ones dressed up as good for you and sold with a *health halo* (insert our angry faces). For example, a pasteurized prepared cheese product and a fiber-spiked, sugar-free snack bar are what we would consider an overly processed food.

Whole food—Food that's close to its natural form or with few ingredients. Like steak—the ingredient is beef. We don't eat perfectly whole foods all the time, as we mentioned. Most of the time, we try to eat mostly whole or low-ingredient foods, but we don't freak out if there's a store-bought cupcake at a birthday party. We're eatin' it!

Real food—Similar to whole food in that it's regular ol' food not laden with artificial stuff or tremendously processed and *definitely not diet food*. Sometimes we use the terms *whole food* and *real food* interchangeably, and there are items that have more than one ingredient and we still consider them to be whole or real foods. For example, if you can buy a whole fat or regular product, we prefer this over something that has been overly processed to be fat-free or low-fat. We need fat (so does baby), and it's tasty.

Baby food—Puréed, and likely jarred, food no longer in its natural form or texture.

Diet—A collection of foods we typically eat.

Dieting—The act of manipulating the body's energy needs via caloric, fat, or other restriction and/or ignoring natural hunger and fullness cues for the sheer purpose of weight loss. Dieting is the opposite of the *Born to Eat* approach. If you're on the diet train as a parent, we've got some great info for you in chapter 10.

Weaning—The process of an infant moving from a sole diet of breastmilk or formula to the incorporation of solid foods for pleasure, nourishment, growth, and development.

Self-feeding—The process that allows baby to use their own hands to feed themselves whole foods similar to what the caregivers are consuming while also choosing how much breastmilk or formula is consumed on demand.

Family meal—A meal at any time of the day where at least one child and one adult are present and eating together at a table.

How to Use This Book

Born to Eat is divided into four parts. Part One will take you through the background of a *Born to Eat* approach, including the background on baby food, the science behind a self-feeding or baby-led approach, and tools for preparing for your *Born to Eat* journey. Part Two has five chapters each devoted to eater stages from the pre-eating beginner to the advanced eater. If you're little one is six months or sixteen months, there's a place to jump right in! Part Three truly brings the *Born to Eat* approach full-circle. It's not just about feeding a baby; it's about a healthy environment for the whole family that fosters body confidence and trust. We'll guide you toward a *Born to Eat* mentality for the adults in the household, help you plan meals, and learn to savor taste and textures as a family. In Part Four, we share our favorite first foods, how to cook and serve them, along with breakfast, lunch, and dinner favorites. We're so excited you're on this journey with us!

> "There is no such thing as a perfect parent. So just be a real one."
> —Sue Atkins

PART 1

THE *BORN TO EAT* FOUNDATION

CHAPTER 1

WE ARE *BORN TO EAT*

> "Parenting is the easiest thing in the world to have an opinion about, but the hardest thing in the world to do."
>
> —Matt Walsh

Leslie and her husband were nervous walking into the pediatric specialist's office. The last time they were there, their little one, CC, was four months old and getting her upper lip tie evaluated. But at this visit, they were preparing for a lecture on common feeding practices. They were breaking the mold, going against the grain, and not following the conventional norms of introducing solids to an infant. Their daughter was about seven months old now and eating solid foods at the family table. She was trying and eating the same foods that Leslie and her husband were eating. They both expected to be scolded as they waited to tell the doctor how they were feeding CC without purées or baby food. Instead of a lecture about purées and textures, he said, "Why would I have a problem with that? That's how most the world feeds their children." Leslie and her husband just looked at each other in disbelief and excitement.

Nothing has ever made so much sense to us. Humans have been around for thousands of years. We've not only thrived, but we've flourished. All without baby food. Think about it: the human race has made it this far, largely on whole foods. Only in recent decades have we begun overthinking and overprocessing our foods, which has led to chronic dieting, chronic disease, and epic confusion about the best way to feed ourselves and our families. We, as humans, are *Born to Eat*. It's an innate skill that has simply been overcomplicated and underappreciated. It seems only natural to start at the beginning—with our babies. For the most part, when developmentally ready, they can eat what we eat and hopefully become healthy, happy eaters, enjoying whole foods in the process.

> Only in recent decades have we begun overthinking and overprocessing our foods, which has led to chronic dieting, chronic disease, and epic confusion about the best way to feed ourselves and our families.

Many countries, aside from the United States, feed their babies this way once they're physically and developmentally ready. And parents feed using a whole food or baby self-feeding approach without fear. From birth, babies around the globe are fed in a variety of manners, whether it be the breast, a bottle, pre-masticated food (pre-chewed and fed to baby), food from the hands of a caregiver, or using a spoon. Many cultures around the world feed their babies what the family is eating and in the same manner. There are also places in the world where families don't make or have access to baby foods, yet their children are still fed and grow.

The use and production (or invention) of commercial baby food became popular during the late 1920s. There had been no major need for special foods for infants since recommendations in those times were not to give solids until around one year of age. As women entered the workforce, there was a greater demand for a convenient way to feed their children. The age recommendations to introduce solids became younger and younger, some even just weeks after birth. By the 1950s, commercial baby food was mainstream and touted to be a more contemporary way of feeding. It was often marketed as a superior food to what parents could make at home. Ultimately, commercial baby food became a convenience item marketed to the modern woman. What parent wouldn't want to do the best by their baby? The creation and existence of baby food today makes sense to us, and we understand why people chose to use certain baby food products. Parents and caregivers are busy and want what's best for their children.

But what if we were to hit rewind? What if we returned to an era of no baby food, where the foods our infants ate were just the same foods that were a part of the whole family's diet? What if we, the parents, provided foods to the family without fussing over the freezer trays or expensive pastel blenders? What if this meant the possibility of better body trust and a healthy relationship with food for a lifetime? That time is now. This is the *Born to Eat* approach. We believe that it's less confusing, possibly more nutritious, and even—get ready—easier in the long run than contemporary and conventional advice.

> We're aren't saying that people who've used baby food did something wrong. We're saying there's another way.

We believe there's really no such thing as baby food, or kid food for that matter. Clever marketing and restaurant menus try their best to convince us as parents that packaged and, much of the time, overly-processed foods are best for our kids. It's also convinced us that kids just don't like so-called adult, or normal, foods. Many believe it's normal for kids to live on chicken fingers, French fries, and mac-n-cheese since they simply don't have the taste for vegetables. While we find those foods appealing at times for all ages, this is very far from the truth, and we're excited to correct that notion. Don't get us wrong—there are some great, baby-friendly convenience foods that we use while on the go or traveling, but for most of our everyday meals, our little ones eat what we eat. It's the *Born to Eat* way. There are ways we have modified our food preparation to be more baby-friendly, such as ditching foods with loads of added sugar or salt, and preparing or portioning the baby plate differently from ours. But, on the whole, what we make for dinner is what the family eats. And our clients have been very happy to learn that there are no short-order cooks in *Born to Eat* homes.

> "What I realized is that the approach was very natural for both my girls. I believe it was the best for my family because it saves time and money, and it enhances our interest in our baby's eating—saying 'This is grandma's tuna salad' meant more to me than 'Here's the puréed chicken.'"
> —Rebecca Scritchfield, registered dietitian, food and fitness expert, and author of *Body Kindness*

Simply put, once developmentally appropriate, baby is allowed to self-feed the foods of the family while still using on-demand breast or formula feedings. This leaves being spoon-fed purées completely out of the process since baby is self-feeding. We, Leslie and Wendy Jo, often use the terms *baby-led weaning* and *self-feeding* interchangeably. There's some debate about the terms, but let's not get hung up on that. The *Born to Eat* approach starts with baby self-feeding with safety precautions and nutrition advice along the way. Although self-feeding is considered nontraditional, it isn't a new way of feeding. It's been used for thousands of years.

The term *baby-led weaning* (BLW) was first coined by Gill Rapley and Tracey Murkett in their book *Baby-Led Weaning: The Essential Guide to Introducing Solid Foods*. We both found this book very helpful and we were glad to have had it for a resource. Dr. Rapley has paved the way for a natural approach to feeding that focuses on foods of the family table. Her book has spurred an emerging body of research, as well. Being the foodies and nutrition therapists we are, we knew we wanted to add to these amazing feeding resources and demonstrate how a feeding approach can impact not just what babies are eating, but *their relationship with food and body for a lifetime.*

Like we mentioned, *Born to Eat* isn't just an approach to feeding using a baby-led style or self-feeding techniques—it's a philosophy. As you've gathered by now, we believe humans are *Born to Eat.* There's a drive to eat as soon as a baby is born. Just watch how a newborn will bob for the breast or bottle within minutes of birth. We are born with innate skills that guide our desire for nourishment. In the early years of life, we can take something so beautifully designed in nature and support it through nurture likely leading to a healthy, lifelong relationship with food and our bodies.

The *Born to Eat* philosophy starts with a self-feeding baby but encompasses so much more. We feel that any parent, adult, or child can embrace the *Born to Eat* key values:

1. Eat whole food as often as possible, from the developmentally appropriate infant through adulthood
2. Honor and support self-regulation of body nourishment
3. When possible, eat as a family
4. Be present and purposeful with food
5. Support a healthy body through body confidence, trust, and gratitude

Let's break these down a bit . . .

Eat Whole Food as Often as Possible

We often use the terms *whole* and *real* interchangeably, but we try to stick to the term *whole*. In our respective offices, we find ourselves explaining what it means *to us*. We are born to eat real, whole food, yet real food isn't all that apparent. We are bombarded with health messages and products that scarcely resemble the whole food it once was. The most common, and deceiving, buzzwords could be *healthy, wheat,* and *thin*. It seems you could put any of the three descriptors on a box and sell most anything. At first glance, we tend to believe what we hear and read is usually true, especially when we respect the source. Why would manufacturers, health professionals, or the media tell us anything but the truth? The short answer is to sell a product. Don't get us wrong—they're plenty of caring, up-to-date professionals and quality products out there—but ultimately, we believe that *what you chew is up to you* (you're going to see that phrase a lot). We could go on and on, but these are our general guidelines for a more whole-food way of eating.

Our bottom line definition for whole, or real, food, is "a food that hasn't been highly processed or made specifically as a diet product or fat-altered food." Now all foods are processed in some way to make it to our grocery stores, but when we're talking about highly processed foods, we mean something that has lots of refined ingredients and additives. A good example is a snack bar, perceived as healthy with an unheard of amount of fiber that will likely result in spending the rest of the afternoon hiding or in the bathroom. We say, if you want more fiber, add more fruits and vegetables, not something manufactured to have fiber and sold with a *health halo*.

When possible, we recommend selecting foods that are whole or single-ingredient foods as often as you can (many of them don't have nutrition facts labels at all). A few examples are tomato (ingredient: tomato), steak (ingredient: beef), eggs (ingredient: eggs), or almond (ingredient: almond). You get the gist. Think about shopping the perimeter of the grocery store for fresh, whole foods like produce, meat, dairy items, bulk items like nuts, oats, quinoa, etc. Although there are many whole foods throughout the grocery, like in the canned and freezer sections, we like to start with the perimeter.

Next, we try to buy items we can't or don't make with few ingredients. For example, we don't make butter, but we sure eat loads of it. Yes, you read that right. Butter. Ingredients: cream and salt. We're totally down with that! A few examples of low-ingredient items would be cheeses, yogurt, nut butters, crackers with few ingredients, and so on.

We also like to choose whole, regular-fat foods. We're not sure that the whole fat debate will ever be over—whole fat versus low-fat versus no-fat. The *Born to Eat* team chooses whole fat yogurts, whole fat cheeses, and whole fat milks. We don't buy defatted peanut butter, fat-free cheese (it's shiny—ew), or low-fat breads. Fat is crucial for development, hormone production, and even aids in our body's natural capacity to regulate hunger and fullness. Low-fat and fat-free products are generally full of things like added sugar and other fillers to make up for the flavor power of the missing fat. This often results in more processing and additives and possibly eating far more because we're not satisfied. We use the real deal when available and feel that although conventional recommendations haven't caught up (and there are many possible reasons for that), the research is there to support using whole, regular foods.[1] Professor of pediatrics at Harvard Medical School and Boston Children's Hospital David Ludwig wrote this in an article on CNN.com.[2] "Responding to new evidence, the 2015 USDA Dietary Guidelines lifted the limit on dietary fat, unofficially ending the low-fat diet era. But you'd never know it, because a full accounting of this failed experiment has not been made." So, we're going to stick to full-fat, regular products whenever possible.

> ## We don't *do* diet food.

We love to say eat real food, but don't get crazy! It's a *most of the time* way of eating, or 80/20 approach with the foods we eat. This means that, most of the time, you plan for and fuel with high-quality whole foods. So when you're at that birthday party having a cupcake or a slice of pizza you didn't make, it's not a problem. We sit down and enjoy that cupcake, too! However, if you find yourself digging through the trash at said party to inspect the ingredients on the cupcake package—that's what we mean by crazy. Now this is not talking about a parent of a child with allergies. Rest assured, if we were at *that* party, we'd be digging in the trash along with you!

Honor and support self-regulation of body nourishment

We've all experienced feelings of physical hunger. Our stomach may growl, we may feel a bit off, or we may have this gentle sensation of emptiness. It's also safe to say that most people have experienced being satisfied, or getting just enough at a meal and feeling the need for more food a couple hours later. On the flip-side, many, if not all of us, have probably experienced that overly, almost sick, full feeling—like Thanksgiving after dessert. Watching an infant turn away from food, push food away, or purse her lips to refuse food is a visual sign of this amazing, innate self-regulation skill. This is our favorite *no* because they are demonstrating that they're tuning into their bodies, and we are honoring their fullness. Supporting a child with self-feeding, or allowing the infant to honor their own hunger and fullness cues, is called *responsive feeding*. We feel it can support lifelong trust in one's body along with feeding competence.

In our fast-paced and, unfortunately, dieting-obsessed society, we often ignore and distrust our own intuitive cues to feed ourselves. We believe in fostering self-regulation in our children and as adults even if we have to relearn it. There's no room for dieting or restrictive behaviors in a *Born to Eat* home.

> We don't believe in or recommend dieting. Dieting is a predictor of disordered eating practices and becoming overweight. We are *Born to Eat*, not born to withhold nourishment from our bodies.

When Possible, Eat as a Family

In this busy world of ours, we all struggle to sit down, slow down to take a breath, and or even savor a meal. But we need to. We have to. Our health, and our family's health, depend on it. Family meals model for our children how to eat, how to behave at the table, and how to try new foods. At an early age, babies watch parents hold silverware, chew food, and savor (and dislike) what they're eating. It's important for babies to watch their caregivers chew, drink from a cup, use a fork, enjoy flavors, and listen to them describe their foods. We understand the busy life, especially if you have multiple children; however, when at all possible, take a seat at the table, pause between each bite, describe to your children what you taste, and enjoy the blessings of a family meal. And there are many. There are numerous reasons to make family meals a priority, and many of them are far greater than just eating food. We'll talk more about that in chapter 10.

Be Present and Purposeful with Food

We believe the food we choose to eat is worth our full attention. When we're present with our food, we can appreciate how it makes us feel. It can make us experience pleasure with taste or texture and then satisfied when we've had enough. If we're present, which means no distractions like the television, emailing, social media, games, etc., it allows us to truly enjoy food, both physiologically and psychologically. We also believe that part of the satisfaction component of eating is to experience pleasure, whether it is to satisfy hunger or excite our taste buds. Being purposeful with food means spending some time to plan eating experiences like meals and snacks. You don't have to get all spreadsheet on us, but it's a good idea to know what's on the menu for dinner. It can impact eating and feeding choices all day long.

A little planning can allow for learning the many aspects of food, such as the nourishment certain foods provide, as well as appreciating and accepting a variety of flavors. Is the food spicy, sweet, smoky, bitter, or tart? So often, we go through a meal and never give a moment's thought as to what we're really tasting—not just eating, but truly tasting the food in front of us. *This* is presence with food. We're consistently coaching our clients to tune out of their jobs when possible and actually take a lunch. We frequently recommend moving away from the television or computer screen to tune into the food so we can experience and taste the food in front of us. On the flipside, it's just as important that we give ourselves permission to step away from a food if it really isn't that satisfying. That can only be accomplished when we're present with our food and the eating experience.

We're excited to share our three-bite food exploration activity in chapter 13, which will walk you through how to tune into your food so you can share it with your little ones. The earlier babies begin to experience flavors and textures, the greater the likelihood they'll try new foods in the future. And we don't believe that *gross* and *yucky* are food descriptors. Our presence and purpose with foods help model and empower our little ones to trust their own self-regulation skills and seek the pleasure of food to satisfy physiological hunger.

Support a Healthy Body through Body Confidence, Trust, and Gratitude

It's hard to ever feel like you're on a healthy path if you believe there's something wrong with how your body works. Like we've mentioned, we're born with skills we need to regulate our bodies. Not feeling able to self-regulate, either as a result of dieting or simply not paying attention to our food, can undermine our body confidence over time. This is the ultimate setup for a very unhealthy relationship with food and our bodies.

We want to make every effort to nip that from infant feeding going forward, and that's why we think the *Born to Eat* approach, which includes the entire family, can make such an impact. When we have confidence that our bodies have what it takes to self-regulate things like the need for food (hunger), the cue to stop eating (satiety), or the need for sleep (getting tired), we don't look for external ways to control our bodies. Having this type of body confidence early in life lays the foundation of body trust. When we trust that our bodies can guide us, we aren't as likely to seek external means of control (like dieting and dieting behaviors) because we've had years of experience of our bodies doing just what they were meant to do—self-regulate.

As parents and caregivers, it's important to foster that inner trust in our infants and children, whether that means letting them stop eating after only a couple bites of food or being up front about what's in front of them. We also have an honesty policy when it comes to eating and food. Trust is crucial to any relationship, and that includes the ones we have with food and our bodies. We're not going to tell you to hide foods or be deceptive about what you're putting on the plate; this doesn't allow for a trusting relationship with food and can sabotage the child-caregiver relationship down the road. Now, we aren't telling you to sit your six-month-old down and tell them about every ingredient in the food. But as our little ones grow, there's nothing wrong with describing to them what they're eating and all the cool stuff it can do in their bodies. We don't have to assume they're not going to like something (like vegetables) and add a minuscule amount to a recipe. That's not what we'd consider a win and won't earn their trust in feeding.

> **Trust is crucial to any relationship, including the one we have with food and our bodies.**

When we begin to understand what the food in front of us can do for our bodies, we have an opportunity to also teach and express gratitude. Gratitude for what we have in front of us—like a warm meal, family and friends, a table to eat at, or a variety of foods—can give us and our kids a positive perspective around food. Gratitude doesn't stop at the dinner table, but it's a wonderful place for it to start. Practicing gratitude helps us appreciate our amazing bodies, and how we digest and utilize nutrients from every bite of food we eat. The energy we gain from food is what fuels our lives. It supports our play, going down a slide, jumping up and down, helping others, learning, reading a bedtime story, or giving a giant hug. Practicing gratitude is a part of the *Born to Eat* approach.

Both of us are grateful. So very grateful. We're grateful that we've used, curated, and reaped the benefits of the *Born to Eat* approach in our own lives. And we're grateful that you are holding *Born to Eat* in your hands right now. It's our hope you'll share in the joys of the *Born to Eat* approach.

Chapter 1 References

1. Patty W. Siri-Tarino, Qi Sun, Frank B. Hu, and Ronald M. Krauss, "Meta-analysis of prospective cohort studies evaluating the association of saturated fat with cardio-vascular disease," *Am J Clin Nutr* March 2010 vol. 91 no. 3 535–546, doi: 10.3945/ajcn.2009.27725

2. David Ludwig, "Doctor: Low-fat Diets Stuffed with Misconceptions," CNN.com, October 6, 2016, accessed October 6, 2016, http://www.cnn.com/2016/10/05/opinions/debate-low-fat-diet-ludwig/index.html.

CHAPTER 2

BENEFITS OF THE SELF-FEEDING APPROACH

Wendy Jo watched her little girl, beneath a yogurt-smothered face, work on chewing, eating, and gagging on a cooked pear wedge. Talk about nerve-racking! Little A made some gagging noises (thank goodness), had a full gag effect, spit out the pear, and then proceeded to grab her next piece. Meanwhile, Wendy Jo was sitting on her hands with her eyes glued to Little A, trying to coach her to *chew, chew, chew.* Even as a trained professional in food and nutrition, Wendy Jo still had to calm her nerves, hide her own fear, and give her daughter the opportunity to learn on her own. This would not be the last time in life she'd have to watch her daughter navigate challenges on her own, so perhaps it was a good thing Wendy Jo started training

herself right away. The good news is that with every meal and every bite, Little A gained confidence and skill, and so did her mama.

Feeding ourselves can be tricky at times. Feeding our kids the right food, at the right time, with the right texture—that can be downright overwhelming. We'd be lying if we said it wasn't scary for us, even with our nutrition backgrounds. They're our little ones—our beautiful and amazing kids. We want them to be healthy, safe, and well. That's why we both decided to study and use the baby-led style or self-feeding approach with our infants. In our study, we found that not only can this approach be an appropriate feeding method for most infants, but it may also be associated with lower maternal anxiety about the feeding process.[1] Yes, please! We both signed up for less anxiety!

Babies take their time. They're watching you eat, and learning with every bite. If a person is constantly in a rush or finds themselves distracted during mealtimes, it could spell trouble down the road. If your skin crawls when a mess occurs, or you jump with every piece of dropped food, you may want to either rescue a dog (the best food vacuum cleaners on the planet) or perhaps choose a different feeding approach. Of course  we're kidding, but the truth is this approach is messy at first. In our own experiences, we've found that kids who've used this approach have better use and control of their spoons and forks at an early age. The mess is huge, but short-lived, and our dogs sure enjoy the treats their two-legged siblings drop their way.

Beyond the mess potential, you can find some information out there that scares parents and discourages starting the baby-led or self-feeding process. We discovered it in the midst of supporting self-feeding with our own kids as practicing and experienced professionals. It was important for us to remember that change isn't necessarily wrong, but it's almost always scary.

> Research suggests that most healthy full-term infants do not need the addition of complementary foods until about six months of age.[2] When developmentally appropriate, most infants appear to be ready for self-feeding, or baby-led weaning.

Benefits of the Self-Feeding Approach

Whether we're talking to parents or professionals or reading the research, the main fears for using this approach are choking, the potential to miss the key nutrient iron, and slower growth patterns.[3] Let's face it, there are some challenges when it comes to baby-led weaning, just like with any type of feeding. We feel the benefits far outweigh the potential risks, or concerns, and we're going to address each of those concerns using the emerging research on this feeding method. It's also important to note that emerging research has *not validated* those possible risks. They're simply concerns or fears, albeit valid ones, that we will address.

The potential benefits don't just end at food for the family (and the family pet). We feel that using a self-feeding approach is more economical and could even have a positive societal impact, as well. If you're like us, you probably like to save money, you want to buy foods that feed the family (not just baby), you'd absolutely want to skip out on being a short-order cook, and you want to foster feeding skills and body confidence in your child. And, if you're like us, baby-led weaning or a self-feeding approach may be the perfect fit for you and your family.

> It's not just that a self-feeding, or baby-led, approach makes incredible sense to us; it's that emerging levels of research suggest that an approach like this has the potential for lifelong benefits around eating and food acceptance.[4]

At first, some of the benefits seem superficial: less time in the kitchen, not spending money on commercial baby food products, or having a less selective, or picky, eater. However, self-fed babies stand to have even greater benefits when it comes to health and wellness. Having a child who is confident in trying new foods and textures or who is more in tune to hunger and fullness cues means that child is less likely to overeat. We believe this feeding method supports the self-regulating eater by allowing the development of body trust with responsive feeding. Because of this, there is the potential for fewer body and weight concerns in the future. Let's dive in with the benefits of the approach and we'll weave in addressing those concerns as we go.

Improved Feeding Skills and Confidence

The self-feeding approach can promote the learning of chewing before swallowing. From the start, babies who self-feed chew or gum food first, then swallow. By doing so, they learn to recognize their gag reflex and continue chewing before swallowing. A baby who is being spoon-fed and starts with purées is likely learning to swallow first without the opportunity to practice managing foods or textures at their own pace. Additionally, the spoon-feeding process doesn't allow for exploration of baby's own normal and maturing gag reflex, particularly if the caregiver is in control of the spoon.

> "There is neither rational nor research to support the use of purées or spoon-feeding for normal, healthy six-month-old babies. Babies of this age are keen to be independent and to use the skills that they are developing. Six-month-olds who resist being spoon-fed are displaying normal behavior and following their instincts, not being difficult."
>
> —Gill Rapley, PhD, *Community Practitioner*, June 2011, Volume 84, Number 6

Dr. Gill Rapley, coauthor of the book *Baby-Led Weaning*, suggests that the critical phase for chewing development is from six to nine months of age.[5] This is when many babies are still eating fully puréed foods. If the baby is not introduced to more solid textures during that critical chewing development stage, they may become toddlers who are more difficult to feed. We also interviewed pediatric speech therapist and feeding specialist Jacqueline Henry, MA, CCC-SLP, about this approach. Not only does she use aspects of baby-led weaning with her feeding clients, especially self-feeding and food exploration, but she used it with her daughter, as well. Jacqueline suggests that using a self-feeding approach has many benefits when baby is developing oral-motor function, like increased exposure to a variety of textures and self-management of those textures for a more efficient and safe swallow in the future. She also proposes that this approach to feeding allows a more natural progression and maturation of the gag reflex that normally shifts from the front of the tongue toward the back of the tongue. Jacqueline has used self-feeding and baby-led weaning methods with many infants and even those who have some feeding difficulties and developmental delays. She suggests, and we support, that it's important to be open-minded about the feeding approach for every child, even if that means using self-feeding strategies, spoon-feeding strategies, or a combination of both to meet the needs of the child.

Benefits of the Self-Feeding Approach

One of the primary concerns with the baby-led weaning method (or any feeding method, really) is choking. Choking is not something we, or any health professional, take lightly. And across the board, this is the most common fear we hear from fellow parents and health professionals. It's important to note that many parents are unsure of the difference between a normal gag reflex and a choking event. We get how scary it can be just to watch your child gag the first couple of times. We both had to sit on our hands as our babies learned to navigate through a gag. However, it's critical as a parent of a newborn, toddler, or child to know the difference between choking and gagging. We'll clear up those differences in the next chapter. In cases where choking was reported, regardless of the feeding strategy, it was almost always related to specific foods. In chapter 5, we'll list foods that have been noted to increase the risk for choking and textures that may pose a problem. As we progress, we'll even suggest when to introduce them. Feeding our little ones requires time and presence, no matter the feeding method.

It's not just parents who are cautious about this approach. In one study assessing the attitudes of healthcare professionals and mothers toward baby-led weaning, researchers found that some healthcare professionals believed there may be benefits of baby-led weaning, such as supporting self-regulation, yet they still had an attitude of concern about the potential increased risk of choking, iron deficiency, and lower intakes.[6] However, few of those healthcare professionals had actual involvement or experience with the baby-led weaning approach. On the other hand, the parents who successfully used this method reported no major concerns and suggested that they would highly recommend it to other parents. A negative attitude toward, or inexperience with, the method doesn't make it an invalid option. Like the parents in the study, we felt it was worth exploring and using with our own children. Thank goodness, all of the pediatricians and pediatric specialists we encountered through our journeys did, as well.

Emerging research is helping calm some of these fears. A new study published in *Pediatrics*, the official journal of the American Academy of Pediatrics, suggests that infants using a supported baby-led weaning approach were *no more likely* to choke than infants using more traditional feeding methods.[7] Any feeding method can result in choking, but parents can be educated to help reduce the risk. We acknowledge as parents and nutrition professionals that every child is different, temperamentally and developmentally, and will learn and grow at a different pace. As a parent, it will be up to you and those in your circle of trust to make that call for your little one. Both of us started with whole foods where our babies self-fed; however, we also allowed our babies to self-feed purée-like foods such as yogurt, cream of wheat, oatmeal, and applesauce. We also watched our babies work through gags, luckily, without incidents of choking while using this feeding approach.

The Potential for Fewer Weight Concerns

As we mentioned earlier, one concern about the baby-led style or self-feeding approach is a slowed growth pattern or lower weight-gain progression. We're not compelled to believe this is necessarily a bad or good thing. While baby is being allowed to self-regulate and learning to eat, we believe that the growth pattern could be exactly on course for that particular child (providing they're developmentally appropriate for self-feeding). Just like adults, babies come in all shapes and sizes, and that's normal. So we're not sold on this particular concern.

While we don't believe that weight is a good indicator of health or healthy behaviors in adults or children, we understand the necessity of weight as a benchmark for measuring growth and development in infants and children. One study that noted the concern that babies using the baby-led weaning style of feeding had slower weight gain or lower body mass indexes (BMI) also reported that the infants who were spoon-fed gained weight at an above-average rate.[8] Just like we don't use the number on the scale as a predictor of one's health, we don't believe the BMI is a useful tool for that either. The BMI is a measure of one's height in relation to weight. It does not take into account one's actual body composition. It may be a useful tool for studying populations but not necessarily for making individual recommendations, whether for an adult, a child, or an infant.

Across the studies we reviewed, there was a common reporting that, regardless of how baby is fed, via spoon-feeding or through a self-feeding style, introducing solids or complementary foods too early (at or before four months of age) may result in an increased risk for childhood weight concerns. The American Academy of Pediatrics and the World Health Organization recommend to start complementary feeding *around* six months of age when the infant is developmentally appropriate and the gut is mature enough to accept solids. We recommend starting a self-feeding approach at the same time using the same developmental markers that we'll cover in chapter 5.

According to the Feeding Infants and Toddlers Study (FITS, 2002), developmentally appropriate infants given the opportunity to self-regulate their energy intake will do so.[9] We feel that infants using this approach not only typically excel in food variety, eating skill confidence, and self-regulation,[10] but they may also struggle less with weight concerns later in life. As nutrition therapists and registered dietitians, we've seen what not having the ability to self-regulate or trust one's body can do to a person. We feel using this approach can help foster lifelong body trust—a key *Born to Eat* value.

The Possibility for Better Nutritional Quality

Utilizing another *Born to Eat* key value, eating whole food as often as possible, from the developmentally appropriate infant through adulthood, may allow for better overall nutrition quality. Although some convenience foods have their place in our diets and homes, highly processed items may not be best for our daily consumption. We eat those foods sometimes but feel that they're best reserved for times when we need something super-fast and convenient—not our first line of defense. Now don't get us wrong, we still believe there are some great convenience foods that are real, whole, and low-ingredient foods. Some of those are frozen vegetables, canned vegetables, pre-chopped vegetables, pre-made dough, rotisserie chicken, and so forth. We like to make or buy many fun sauces, too. We promise eating more whole food doesn't mean going to live on a farm and cultivating it all yourself. We live in the real world too. That's why we recommend and use some great food products that help all of us get dinner on the table versus eating out or using totally boxed or prepared processed meals. And Leslie's motto just happens to be *eat real food, feel real good*™—but don't get crazy.

> We promise eating more real, whole food doesn't mean going to live on a farm and cultivating it all yourself. We live in the real world, too.

One of the main concerns with the baby-led weaning method is potential for iron deficiency when beginning complementary foods. According to the World Health Organization's official website, "the transition from exclusive breastfeeding to family foods—referred to as complementary feeding—typically covers the period from 6–24 months of age."[11] Generally, approximately six month of age is when a breastfed baby has possibly depleted their available iron stores deposited in the last trimester of pregnancy and must add iron-rich foods into their diet. The amount of actual milk feedings shouldn't decrease when solid foods are introduced around six months of age. This is why the term is *complementary* feedings. While formula-fed babies still get iron from their formula, starting complementary foods with iron-rich options provides other key nutrients,

as well. Regardless of the milk source, we believe this is the next step. And, don't fret! We'll arm you with a list of foods in chapter 5 along with easy recipes that will help you get iron-rich foods in front of the whole family.

For years, many have recommended giving infants iron-fortified infant cereal as a first food. This is based on tradition and *not* medical evidence. Many of these recommendations have lingered from previous guidelines that included feeding infants at approximately four months old when a purée (which isn't a solid) was needed due to the lack of chewing and feeding skills. Given that developmentally appropriate six-month-olds can accept prepared solid foods, there's no reason they can't have foods naturally high in iron like beef and egg yolks. Parents embracing this approach can provide these foods as daily options.

Nutrient quality isn't just an iron issue. For example, if a family struggles to get in ample protein or a nutrient-dense diet, it's likely the vitamins and minerals those missing foods provide are being left out of baby's diet, as well. If a family doesn't plan meals, it's possible convenience items will be the most common food selected. However, planning to use a self-feeding approach may ensure that baby is getting the necessary nutrients; just the simple act

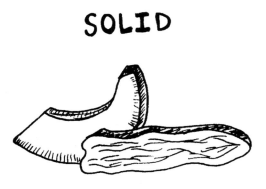

of planning and preparing to add these complementary foods may assist the whole family in eating better with more balanced meals.

As moms, and nutrition professionals, we want what's best for our children and clients. We feel that the *Born to Eat* approach allows for feeding skill development more quickly than beginning with a puréed-only phase and that the infants who are self-feeding are likely to have greater eating confidence and trust. When eating based on their own internal regulation systems, they learn to eat just enough for their bodies.

Overall, we feel this approach can help prevent dieting behavior for the whole family, which could help prevent a lifetime of body distrust and weight concerns. By honoring self-regulation, an innate skill, and focusing on a whole food foundation from the developmentally appropriate infant through adulthood, we can foster healthier children and families using the *Born to Eat* philosophy.

The *Born to Eat* team wants this for your baby, your family, and our own families. We want this for our society. Body trust and confidence shouldn't be uncommon. This is why *Born to Eat* is not just about self-feeding; it's a movement toward a healthier future of body confident adults and children.

Chapter 2 References

1. Ellen Townsend, Nicola J. Pitchford, "Baby knows best? The impact of weaning style on food preferences and body mass index in early childhood in a case-controlled sample," *BMJ Open* 2012;2:e000298, doi:10.1136/bmjopen-2011-000298.

2. Sonya L. Cameron, Anne-Louise M. Heath, Rachael W. Taylor, "How Feasible Is Baby-Led Weaning as an Approach to Infant Feeding? A Review of the Evidence," *Nutrients* 4(11) (2012): 1575–1609, doi:10.3390/nu4111575.

3. Lisa Daniels, Anne-Louise M. Heath, Sheila M. Williams, Sonya L. Cameron, Elizabeth A. Fleming, Barry J. Taylor, Ben J. Wheeler, Rosalind S. Gibson, Rachael W. Taylor, "Baby-Led Introduction to SolidS (BLISS) study: a randomised controlled trial of a baby-led approach to complementary feeding," *BMC Pediatrics* 15 (2015): 179, doi:10.1186/s12887-015-0491-8.

4. See Reference 1.

5. Gill Rapley, "Baby-led weaning: transitioning to solid foods at the baby's own pace," *Community Practitioner* 84 (2011): 20–3, date accessed Oct. 4, 2016.

6. Sonya L. Cameron, Anne-Louise M. Heath, Rachael W. Taylor, "How Feasible Is Baby-Led Weaning as an Approach to Infant Feeding? A Review of the Evidence," *Nutrients* 4(11) (2012): 1575–1609, doi:10.3390/nu4111575.

7. Louise J. Fangupo, Anne-Louise M. Heath, Sheila M. Williams, Liz W. Erickson Williams, Brittany J. Morison, Elizabeth A. Fleming, Barry J. Taylor, Benjamin J. Wheeler, Rachael W. Taylor, "A Baby-Led Approach to Eating Solids and Risk of Choking," *Pediatrics* (September 2016): e20160772, DOI: 10.1542/peds.2016-0772.

8. See Reference 1.

9. Mary Kay Fox, Barbara Devaney, Kathleen Reidy, Carol Razafindrakoto, Paula Ziegler, "Relationship between Portion Size and Energy Intake among Infants and Toddlers: Evidence of Self-Regulation," *Journal of the Academy of Nutrition and Dietetics* Volume 106 , Issue 1 (January 2006): 77–83, DOI: 10.1016/j.jada.2005.09.039

10. Amy Brown and Michelle D. Lee, "Early influences on child satiety-responsiveness: the role of weaning style," *Pediatric Obesity* 10 (2015): 57–66, doi:10.1111/j.2047-6310.2013.00207.x

11. "Appropriate complementary feeding," *e-Library of Evidence for Nutrition Actions (e-LENA)* http://www.who.int/elena/titles/complementary_feeding/en/, date accessed Oct. 4, 2016.

CHAPTER 3

BORN TO EAT BUILDING BLOCKS

> "It's not what you do for your children, but what you have taught them to do for themselves, that will make them successful human beings."
>
> —Ann Landers

Our friend, Julie, said that her experience with self-feeding was one of fear and chickening out. She wished she had a better story to share. With baby number two on the way, she's planning to do things differently. At the time she was beginning to feed her first daughter, the pediatrician she was seeing was very negative about the baby-led weaning process (they've since changed). And she didn't know many people who had any experience with it. The first time her daughter gagged, Julie and her husband got scared and immediately threw in the towel. She says that she wishes she would have kept going now, as feeding her daughter and getting her to eat nutritious foods has been a challenge. She says her daughter isn't the worst eater and that she accepts a variety of foods, but she does run into problems when things are mixed together, or part of a family meal or dish, or foods that are seasoned. Her daughter prefers to eat most of her foods separately, making cooking for the family more stressful and challenging. Now she wonders if sticking with the self-feeding process would have made a difference for her daughter and her cooking times.

Julie says it's her hope that baby number two will be different now that she has more confidence with the process. She's watched many friends embrace the approach with so much success. The first time around, she had so many fears and unanswered questions. All those little details kept her worried and prevented her from fully trying the process. She wonders if she would have been able to make it work if she knew the answers to her questions back then. Fear is such a terrible and paralyzing feeling!

Julie, along with many other moms and nutrition professionals, did us the tremendous favor of sharing all of their concerns, fears, and questions. Even though we've counseled parents of young children for years, both before and after having our own kids, we had our own questions through the process, as well. There were no answers in textbooks and many people, both friends and professionals, just passed off the baby-led or self-feeding approach as a fad. We realized that it wasn't a fad or a new thing, given that the whole human race made it this far without baby food.

In the beginning, we were eager for answers, too, just like all the parents we interviewed. We are grateful that these parents, friends, and professionals shared their experiences—the good ones and the not so good ones—because, when we looked at the fears and questions they shared, we realized that the same questions kept coming up over and over again. We knew we had to address them, and we knew that we could.

The As to the Qs

As promised, we've got the answers to these questions. We'll tackle them briefly here. We've got a lot to share with you, so we're going to tell you where to find more answers throughout the chapters of the book as we go.

> "I never would have even thought about skipping puréed baby food and starting with food the family eats if it was not for a friend I trusted who was doing it with her own daughter. I needed someone else's confidence and knowledge to spark my own interest, and my confidence came later—with experience."
> —Rebecca Scritchfield, registered dietitian, food and fitness expert, and author of *Body Kindness*

Top 10 Questions about a Self-Feeding Approach

1. What is the difference between gagging and choking?
2. How often should baby get breast milk or formula? Several moms I know started eliminating nursing sessions and replaced them with solid feeding sessions.
3. How many meals a day should baby get at first?
4. Should we worry about food allergies?
5. Should we introduce only one food at a time? Is there a timeline? When can we start doing little pieces of chopped grapes? How about a forkful of lasagna? When are crackers okay? Toast?
6. Can baby be served mixed food meals?
7. How long should we cook veggies and how soft should they be? For instance, how long should we boil or steam carrots?
8. How do we serve baby portions? Wide/narrow to cut the strips/chunks? How thick should I slice a little piece of steak? How big should the toast slices be?
9. How long should baby sit at a meal to explore, play, or eat her food? I knew I needed to let her be the one to explore and feed herself, but how long should I give her to explore? Sometimes I sat there and no food would actually be eaten. I didn't know how long I should give her for each meal.
10. What if my pediatrician has never heard of, or is unsupportive of, baby-led weaning?

Q1: What is the difference between gagging and choking?

We admit this didn't come naturally to us either. It's been decades since we used our gag reflex! It's important to realize the difference between gagging and choking. Knowing this can give you peace of mind and information to determine if your child needs your patience through a gag or immediate assistance in the event of choking. Gagging, whether a silent movement of food or coughing, is a normal and reflexive safety mechanism that pushes food that hasn't been fully chewed or mashed toward the front of the mouth so that it can continue to be chewed and then swallowed. If baby is gagging, her eyes may water, she may cough, sputter, make gagging sounds, be silent yet intently moving food toward the front of her mouth, or may look afraid. Choking, though, is when an object or substance becomes stuck in the throat or windpipe, causing the blockage of airflow. If baby is choking, it's unlikely she'll be able to make sounds and will not be able to effectively move air. When infants are eating while reclined, they're at greater risk for choking. It's unlikely baby will have a choking episode if safe self-feeding practices are in place; however, it's imperative that parents are trained in infant CPR procedures. Most hospitals offer this as a part of their prenatal classes. There are also certain foods that tend to be common culprits in a choking event regardless of the feeding method. We'll address those foods in chapter 5.

Q2: How often should baby get breast milk or formula?

When you and baby start the self-feeding process, the foods that you provide are more for skill development than nutrition. While it's important to select foods that provide a nutritional benefit, like being iron- and energy-rich, the sole source of nutrition for baby is still breast milk or formula. Foods added during this time are only supplemental to a milk-based diet, and for this reason, they're called complementary foods. On-demand breast milk or formula feedings should continue until baby reaches one year along with their self-fed foods from the family diet.

Q3: How many meals a day should baby get at first?

We recommend starting with one meal per day. You can decide which meal of the day that is. It depends on the times of day your baby is most alert and eager to eat. Wendy Jo started Miss A with breakfast while Leslie started CC with lunch. Once your baby seems eager to eat more, add another meal with the family and increase as needed. Around eight months old, baby could be having three meals per day, and by ten months, your infant may be moving on to three meals and two to three snacks per day. Their stomachs are very small, so we have to adjust our idea of portions. One to three tablespoons of food may be an appropriate amount for each meal. Some babies may eat more, some babies eat less. Let baby be the guide.

Q4: Should we worry about food allergies?

The baby-led weaning approach can still be followed if there's a concern about food allergies. If you have a family history of food allergies, it's a good idea to discuss introducing solid foods with your pediatrician. Emerging research and recommendations from the American Academy of Pediatrics suggest that even with a family history of food allergies, high-allergen foods be introduced just like other foods when the child is developmentally appropriate to start solids (around six months old). High-allergen foods include eggs, nuts, dairy, soy, shellfish, and wheat. Some researchers theorize that previous recommendations to withhold high-allergen foods to later in the food introduction process may have contributed to a boom in pediatric food allergies, but there is no clear reason for the rise in allergies. Food allergies are a serious and potentially life-threatening condition. Regardless of whether your child has a food allergy, all parents should consider this given that it's estimated that 1 in every 13 children has a food allergy.[1]

Q5: Should we introduce one food at time? Is there a timeline?

This is a recommendation that came about when it was suggested to start puréed complementary feedings at four months of age—a time when baby's gastrointestinal tract may not have been ready for complementary foods at all. The practice of only giving a baby one food at a time was thought to help spot an intolerance or identify an allergic reaction. Many still recommend this practice, but it does not, however, reduce the risk of an infant developing a food allergy. If there's no family history of allergies and you're aware of the ingredients in the foods your family eats, we feel there is no reason to offer only one or two foods over a couple of days. We literally dove right in. If you're concerned about allergies for your little one, there's no reason you can't slow the process.

Our recommendations are to start the self-feeding journey with appropriately prepared whole foods like avocados, steak, eggs, sweet potatoes, carrots, and broccoli. These single-ingredient whole foods can take the guesswork out if your child happens to not tolerate a food well. In general, we recommend starting with whole foods at home so you know what's on the plate in front of you. Your meals will take shape based on your baby's ability to eat and your typical family menu, but introducing even three foods at a meal should not be an issue. If you feel like baby has a reaction to a food, back off on food introductions and try to isolate the food in question. There really is no timeline unless you've worked with your pediatrician to create one if your infant is at risk for a food allergy.

Q6: Can baby be served mixed food meals?

Using this approach, your baby can be served foods of the family. We hope those foods will have balance and great nutrition for the whole household. Given that the first month or so of offering solid foods is more for skill development with chewing, texture, and swallowing, it's a good idea to stick with more whole individual foods versus mixed food meals. We both provided our little ones with individual components of the family meal and then progressed to mixed meals like lasagna, beef stir-fry, chicken pot pie, or spaghetti and meatballs. Once you feel like your baby is starting to eat more than play or skill build, by all means, serve up your family's favorite mixed dish. We'll guide you through.

Q7: How long should we cook veggies and how soft should they be?

Steaming harder fruits and vegetables initially is best. The addition of water softens the food without making the skin or outer portion of the fruit and vegetable tough. Roasting, which is a great way to cook vegetables, will be best introduced just a bit later, as it can toughen the outer portion of some vegetables. When your baby is self-feeding and exploring the different textures of food, he will learn pretty quickly how to work around the skin of most veggies. Our rule of thumb is to steam until the

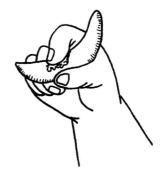

vegetables or fruits are soft enough to gently press with your fingers or the food smashes easily with your tongue pressed to the roof of your mouth. We'll share our preparation tips for these foods in chapter 14.

Q8: How do we serve baby portions?

Too much on a plate is overwhelming for anyone, let alone your baby, who is trying to analyze and assess everything placed in front of him. It's a good idea to have a non-skid plate that is smaller, just for baby. Keep it simple. We recommend serving three foods or three finger-shaped pieces of food at a time. When they appear to want more, place one more piece in front of them.

Q9: How long should baby sit at a meal to explore, play, or eat her food?

However long your meal takes to enjoy and savor. There's no need to rush, and remember, they're observing and learning from you. It could take baby much longer to explore her three food items than it took you to complete your whole meal. Take your time. After about thirty minutes or when they appear to have lost interest, then it's time to change activities. Don't be discouraged if their attention span wanes after only ten minutes. That will get better over time as their feeding skills and eating improve.

Q10: What if my pediatrician has never heard of it?

Several parents we talked to had this experience. Not knowing of baby-led weaning or self-feeding doesn't make it an inappropriate choice; it's simply not known to them at the time. Just like nutrition professionals (us), doctors have to keep up with a tremendous amount of information and may not have had the opportunity to look further into self-feeding and responsive eating. With that said, as parents, we must advocate for our child and do what we feel is best. One study surveying Canadian mothers about their experiences with BLW determined that most mothers relied on other parents and their own instincts for guidance on the process.[2] This is likely because the health professionals they encountered weren't supportive or knowledgeable about the process.

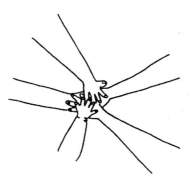

This information also may be helpful to note: The American Academy of Pediatrics' desired behavior resource for physicians is a part of the AAP Health Initiatives. In this resource, the infant food and feeding desired behaviors include fostering self-feeding, which encourages the babies to feed themselves using their hands and spoons along with using a cup.[3] Helping parents understand and recognize hunger and satiety cues are also a suggested desired behaviors of the initiative. These key points of baby-led weaning, written by Dr. Gill Rapley, may help sum up the approach for anyone on baby's support team.

Key Points of Baby-Led Weaning

- ❏ Baby-led weaning refers to the introduction of solid foods using a self-feeding approach, and it is developmentally and nutritionally appropriate for most infants
- ❏ Breastmilk (or formula) should continue to be the main source of nutrition up to one year
- ❏ From six months, babies need to practice the skills involved in self-feeding
- ❏ Provided basic safety rules are followed, self-feeding does not present any greater risk of choking than spoon-feeding
- ❏ This method of feeding during the weaning period has the potential to influence the infant's dietary choices and relationship with food for the remainder of their life

Used with permission from Gill Rapley, PhD & Community Practitioner, *Baby-Led Weaning: Transition to Solid Foods at the Baby's Own Pace* in the *Community Practitioner*, June 2011.

We feel strongly that starting baby with the self-feeding approach can have lifelong benefits. These ideas, or what we term *the building blocks of self-feeding*, are not unique to just the *Born to Eat* team. Fellow moms, dads, friends, professionals, and researchers have shaped the foundation of the *Born to Eat* approach. It's not just about eating. The *Born to Eat* approach is about how this strategy of self-feeding can foster a healthy relationship with foods and a body for a lifetime—and not just for baby.

> We feel that families who use and support the Division of Responsibility in feeding and eating foster body-confident children that grow into adults capable of eating intuitively.

If you're embracing the self-feeding style completely, or using some spoon-feeding along with it, we believe you can cultivate a self-regulating, or responsive, feeder if you follow Ellyn Satter's Division of Responsibility. Ellyn Satter is a renowned dietitian and clinical social worker known for her eating and feeding philosophies, the Satter Feeding Dynamics Model, and the Division of Responsibility in Feeding. The Satter Feeding Dynamics Model is a well-known and well-supported feeding model in the medical and health community. It's considered a best practice by the Academy of Nutrition and Dietetics and the American Academy of Pediatrics among others.[4] The Division of Responsibility in Feeding suggests that there are roles for the parent to support the child's natural ability to eat and self-regulate by providing the foods while allowing the child to decide how much and if they will eat.

> "I had to learn about feeding dynamics, the research on feeding styles, responsive feeding, and eating competence as a parent, and I am grateful that I did. Seeing the transformation in my own home, as well as the growing literature on the health and wellness benefits of eating well, guided by internal cues of hunger and fullness, convinced me that helping children grow up to be competent eaters is preventive medicine."
>
> —Katja Rowell, MD, childhood feeding specialist and author

CHAPTER 3 REFERENCES

1. "Resources for Kids," *Food Allergy Research and Education*, accessed September 20, 2016, http://www.foodallergy.org/resources/kids

2. D'Andrea, Elisa, Jenkins, Kielyn, Mathews, Maria, Roebothan, Barbara, "Baby-led Weaning: A Preliminary Investigation," *Canadian Journal of Dietetic Practice and Research* 77(2) (2016 June): 72–7, doi: 10.3148/cjdpr-2015-045. Epub 2016 Jan 15.

3. "Infant Food and Feeding," *American Academy of Pediatrics*, accessed August 19, 2016, https://www.aap.org/en-us/advocacy-and-policy/aap-health-initiatives/HALF-Implementation-Guide/Age-Specific-Content/Pages/Infant-Food-and-Feeding.aspx

4. "The Satter Feeding Dynamics Model," *Ellyn Satter Institute*, accessed August 5, 2016, http://ellynsatterinstitute.org/other/fdsatter.php

CHAPTER 4

SUPPORT AND THE *BORN TO EAT* COMMITMENT

> "Those who have a strong sense of love and belonging have the courage to be imperfect."
>
> —Brené Brown

Our friend, Nikki, was headed back to work in the midst of her baby-led weaning process. Her daughter was seven months old and exploring a variety of family foods. When she dropped off her daughter at daycare the first day, she found herself explaining the baby-led weaning process along with many justifications. As she jokingly says, "The CWGs (conventional wisdom grannies) just didn't get it, and I felt like they told me they'd support the process, but when I turned and walked out, I just knew they were going to shove a spoon in her mouth."

She was frustrated but knew that spoon-feeding wouldn't ruin her daughter. Many parents and caregivers allow the child to lead by watching the subtle cues babies display when they've had enough—like turning their heads, pursing their lips, or even swatting the spoon away. In her situation, she got the feeling that wouldn't be the case, that the CWGs were going to have her daughter finishing the baby food, down to the last bite, not allowing her to self-regulate. She'd seen it with other infants there. Instead of getting totally frustrated, Nikki reached out to friends and trusted professionals to help her find a balance between her daughter being spoon-fed at preschool and allowed to self-feed using a baby-led approach at home. And, after she discussed her wishes with the staff, and educated them on using spoon-feeding while letting her daughter be the guide of if she ate and how much, it worked. So many of who've gone before us are committed to lifelong learning and are excited to support us in this journey. All you have to do is start the conversation.

> There is no perfect way to do this. It can be done all the way, halfway, or any combination in between. As long as baby leads the way, there are no flops!

It's a Messy (but Amazing) Process

We've mentioned it before—the *Born to Eat* approach is a tad messy. Okay, really messy. We've gotten a lot laughs out of the friends and grandmas that have said there's no way they'd let their babies feed themselves in such a messy manner. We, on the other hand, gave it a shot, embraced the mess (which honestly is short-lived), and have reaped the benefits. These benefits could last a lifetime, which to us, far outweighs the mess. Let's face it—whenever one chooses to allow a baby to self-feed, whether at six months old or one year old, there's going to be discovery, and ultimately a mess. So, either way you get the mess, it's just now or later. At least starting earlier, there's a little less food on the plate to paint the wall.

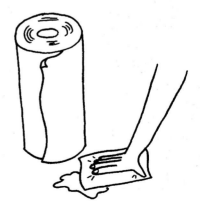

We embraced the mess, bought stock in paper towels (well maybe not, but perhaps we should have), and had to walk our dogs a bit more because of all the flying pasta. All joking aside, we want to give you an idea of how we handle mealtimes with some great feeding tools and tricks. Even between the two of us, we entered the process of baby-led weaning differently. Leslie's little one is older than Wendy Jo's, so there were different tools of the trade at the different times. We've worked together to come up with a list of items that made the messy process less of an issue.

Wendy Jo invested in silicone plates and placemats, which (on some surfaces) sticks to the table, and the Stokke™ Tripp Trapp high chair that scoots directly up to the table. She has a box of burp cloths and little towels she keeps handy for after-dinner wipe downs, and a bottle of cleaning spray for the table and high chair post meals. Miss A wore an IKEA smock (and, technically, she was doing a bit of painting). Additionally, Miss A started her eating adventures with Num Nums™ spoons and Think™ cups. As for floor cleanup, Wendy Jo skipped the vinyl tablecloth, because she has tile beneath her table and two dogs on cleanup duty.

> Miss A had a Bolognese sauce painted face, red streaked hair, and pasta flung across the tile, but she was flanked by two very happy Labradors. Wendy Jo would say that her dogs fell in love with Miss A as soon as she began eating. Love at first bite.

Leslie used a round mat to go under the high chair (with a foot rest) at the dining room table since she had a pretty new rug and fresh paint. The avocado slice that hit the dining room wall blended right in. Luckily, having a box of baby wipes by the high chair made cleaning up CC, and her surroundings, much easier. Even the fresh paint survived without touchups. We had a variety of non-skid plates and great gripping spoons. Our favorite spoons were made by Nuk and even IKEA. Leslie wishes she would have had silicone plates and placemats with her little one.

> Our feeding experts suggest using a high chair with appropriate foot support or a foot rest. Little dangling feet can be quite distracting!

The tools we feel that can help minimize the mess may reduce the mess-induced critics. We have some very clean and tidy family members who really did not enjoy seeing the mess. We had some friends who scoffed that our babies got a daily bath. Then we had some strangers comment what adventurous eaters we had when they watched our little ones dive into their plate of Mexican food while eating out. You've probably already gotten some really great (or not) unsolicited advice. It seems everyone's a critic, whether positive or negative. Regardless, don't forget that this is your family, your baby, and your choice. What you chew (and baby chews), is up to you! We are here to empower you with the real deal, the low-down, the emerging research, and easy recipes to support you and the feeding path you pick for your child. We're on this imperfect journey together!

> The goal is getting baby exposed to self-feeding as soon as developmentally appropriate, and if it takes a few other supportive methods for baby to succeed, then so be it.

One thing is clear—there's definitely enough shaming in our culture. One of greatest examples of mommy or parent shaming around food starts from day one, breast milk or formula. If you choose to breastfeed, formula feed, combo feed, or whatever, someone thinks something isn't right. The same is true for how you're feeding foods to your baby. We feel like you and only you can make the best choice for your baby, using the best information you have. Like we mentioned, you can do this halfway, partially, half-time, or however you need to in your life, just like Nikki did with her daughter. And it's never all unicorns and lollipops. Leslie had serious issues while breastfeeding along with guilt and shame about not feeling like she could provide enough for daughter. Luckily for Leslie, her husband, and her little one, she had an amazing breastfeeding medicine pediatrician on her team. And Dr. Julie always said, "Leslie, don't forget this: rule number one is feed the baby." That's what we're going to help you do.

The goal is getting baby exposed to self-feeding as soon as developmentally appropriate, and if it takes a few other supportive methods for baby to succeed, then so be it. You know what is best for your baby and what your baby is capable of achieving because you see the small changes (or not) in developmental readiness daily. Trust your instincts and go with your gut and mind. When you find yourself in a position where you need support or you feel the need to explain the process to caregivers, we can help. The *Born to Eat* approach starts with a focus on baby self-feeding. We have you covered with two samples advocating for support for you and baby. One addresses a caretaker outside of the home and the other addresses a close friend or family member. You'll find these at the end of this chapter. Please take the liberty to tweak as needed. We've also included a fantastic handout called *Born to Eat* Basics, which is influenced by the *Baby-Led Introduction* to Solids (BLISS) Study: A Randomized Controlled Trial of a Baby-Led Approach to Complementary Feeding. We're positive you'll want to keep it close and copy for caregivers. **You can find the *Born to Eat* Basics tear-out in the back of the book.**

It's Time for the *Born to Eat* Commitment

You didn't see that coming, did you? A commitment? This commitment could change so many things in your baby's life, in your entire family's life, your life, and in our society. The *Born to Eat* commitment is based on the *Born to Eat* values that we've broken down into everyday activities. It's not just a feeding approach; it's a philosophy that could foster body trust, decrease the impact of our diet-crazed culture, cultivate more supportive microcommunities, and help us have peace with our bodies and food. Who doesn't want that?

Let's do this!

I agree:

- To not feel the need to be legalistic or perfect with any feeding method.
- To recognize that what I (and baby) chew is up to me.
- To embrace creativity with food and feeding as a learning tool.
- To realize that my family and I get to decide what foods are best.
- To make my own definition of what whole and real foods mean for my family.
- To not push food on, or restrict food, from my child (or myself).
- To embrace the messy and challenging adventure together.
- To advocate for myself and my child throughout the process.

Cheers to:

- An endless supply of clean towels.
- Excellent stain-removing detergents.
- Babies who self-regulate.
- Babies who turn into children who know how to savor foods.
- Children who listen to their hunger and fullness cues.
- Children who grow into men and women who love and honor their bodies who can then teach their children to do the same.

Welcome to the *Born to Eat* Community. We are so happy you're on this journey with us!

Sincerely,

L & WJ

> ## "Creativity is the best tool for embedding knowledge."
> —Brené Brown

Dear Care Team Member,

Thank you so much for caring for my baby. I have entrusted you with his/her care because I know you care about him/her, too. In the care of **(insert child's name)**, we have a request in regards to feeding styles and approaches. Based on current research, we won't be introducing foods to him/her until about six months old, as there are clear signs of readiness our health professionals want to see before he/she can eat whole foods. We'd love for you to help us take note of these signs of readiness, as we know you are around **(insert child's name)** quite often. These are the signs we are looking for:

- Sits up independently without the use of a high chair or pillow
- No longer thrusts tongue
- Shows interest in eating foods
- Reaches for foods with palm of hand or scooping motion

In addition to waiting a bit longer to start complementary foods, we are using the *Born to Eat* approach, which embraces self-feeding, where **(insert child's name)** is given graspable whole foods and allowed to play with, chew on, and self-feed these foods. We understand this may be a unique approach and would gladly provide more information for you.

Please know that choosing this approach is in no way a criticism of traditional feeding practices. Instead, it's our hope that our child will accept a variety of flavors and textures quickly, trust innate hunger and fullness cues, and be able to self-regulate his/her eating for years to come.

These tips have helped us implement this approach:

- Only serve whole foods (for example, sliced steak, sliced boiled eggs, avocado wedges, roasted carrots, steamed asparagus, raspberries)
- Foods are soft enough to smash gently between two fingers or with the tongue to the top of the mouth
- Very few foods are given at one time (for example, a piece of avocado wedge, 1 steamed soft carrot finger, 3 raspberries, 1 slice of boiled egg) and more is given as needed. This is so she/he is not overwhelmed by too much food on the plate. >>

If you're willing to support us in this approach, we would love your help and encouragement. We know that choking is a concern for all of us no matter the feeding method. We've recently learned to watch and coach through a normal (yet scary) gagging episode without responding with fear. Yet, choking is a life-threatening event that blocks all airflow and sounds. We're confident that in the unlikely event of choking, you would follow the safety procedures to help our child.

If this approach cannot be carried out or safely monitored under your supervision, we ask that our child could be allowed to self-feed traditional baby foods or purées. We have provided a smock to help minimize the mess and will wash this daily for you. Please let us know how we can further help you in the care and support of our child. We appreciate your care, understanding, and support.

Sincerely,

_____ (sign)

Dear Aunt Betty (or Mom, Mother-in-law, family member, friend),

First off, thank you so much for watching your niece (or granddaughter, etc.). We know how much you enjoy this time with **(insert child's name)**, and we appreciate the help tremendously. We wanted to let you know how we are choosing to introduce food to **(insert child's name)**. Based on current research, we won't be introducing foods to him/her until about six months old, as there are clear signs of readiness our health professionals want to see before he/she can eat whole foods. We'd love for you to help us take note of these signs of readiness, as we know you are around **(insert child's name)** quite often.

Here are the signs we are looking for:

- Sits up independently without the use of a high chair or pillow
- No longer thrusts tongue
- Shows interest in eating foods
- Reaches for foods with palm of hand or scooping motion

In addition to waiting a bit longer to start complementary foods, we are using the *Born to Eat* approach, which embraces a self-feeding style, where **(insert child's**

>>

name) is given graspable whole foods and allowed to play with, chew on, and self-feed these foods. We understand this may be a unique approach, and we are excited to talk to you more about it and provide you with the *Born to Eat* book.

Please know that choosing this approach is in no way a criticism of traditional feeding practices. Instead, it's our hope that our child will accept a variety of flavors and textures quickly, trust innate hunger and fullness cues, and be able to self-regulate his/her eating for years to come.

These tips have helped us implement this approach:

- Only serve whole foods (for example, sliced steak, sliced boiled eggs, avocado wedges, roasted carrots, steamed asparagus, raspberries)
- Foods are soft enough to smash gently between two fingers or with the tongue to the top of the mouth
- Very few foods are given at one time (for example, a piece of avocado wedge, 1 steamed soft carrot finger, 3 raspberries, 1 slice of boiled egg) and more is given as needed. This is so she/he is not overwhelmed by too much food on the plate.

These behaviors have been really helpful for us to practice as well:

- refraining from panicking when they work through a gag
- not putting your fingers in his/her mouth when they are working through gagging
- helping to test foods to ensure they are the right texture
- coaching **(insert child's name)** to "chew, chew, chew"
- modeling how to chew by eating the same foods with him/her

Another benefit to this approach is that we do not have to purchase traditional jarred baby foods. **(insert child's name)** can eat whatever we are eating as long as the food is cut in a manageable size and provided in the appropriate texture. As we go through this process of introducing foods, we have helpful lists of age-appropriate foods, textures, recipes, and those that are not appropriate for this stage.

When you are watching your niece (or granddaughter, etc.) you can choose what you feel comfortable with and we will support you. If you'd like to practice this approach with us, we'd love the extra support.

Love,

_____ (sign)

PART 2

THE *BORN TO EAT* BABY AND CHILD

Feeding our little ones can be nerve-racking at first, particularly if you're using a method some consider *nontraditional*. As parents who've embarked on this journey, we divided this part of the book into chapters based on your little one's age and readiness. This is the *start here with this food* part of the book. If you're like us, you like a starting point. We've also classified ages as different levels of eaters like this:

Chapter 5: Begins with your 6-month-old or the Pre-Eating Beginner

Chapter 6: Moves onto your 7- to 8-month-old or the Beginner Eater

Chapter 7: Jumps to your 9- to 12-month-old or the Novice Eater

Chapter 8: Talks toddling with your 12- to 24-month-old or the Pre-Advanced Eater

Chapter 9: Covers the ever-changing 24- to 36-month-old or the Advanced Eater

In each chapter, we discuss readiness based on the skills generally achieved during this time. We also discuss priority nutrients. While the nutrients are important through all stages, there's no need to be overwhelmed by focusing on all of them right at the start. You'll love how we get you started with necessary nutrients from the first bite with ease. Let's start the self-feeding process!

CHAPTER 5

IT'S GO TIME
(6 MONTHS–THE PRE-EATING BEGINNER)

> "The proverb warns that 'You should not bite the hand that feeds you.' But maybe you should, if it prevents you from feeding yourself."
> —Thomas Szasz

At just four months old, Wendy Jo had a little yogi on her hands. Miss A was starting to sit up and getting ready to move out on all fours. At five months to the day, she took her first crawl. She was incredibly interested in food, watching everything Wendy Jo was eating. When Miss A napped, Wendy Jo enjoyed some of her larger meals without the little eyes and hands. Although she wanted to share that first bite of food together very soon, Wendy Jo knew Miss A was not developmentally ready. She had to remind herself that Miss A had her whole life to eat and so she needed to be patient. Wendy Jo decided to sit back and let Miss A's development take place without rushing into anything. Just a few more weeks . . .

Leslie got home from seeing clients one day to hear that six-month CC had smashed some sliced steak and avocado right into her mouth. She sucked all the nutritious juices out of the steak and smashed the avocado—some in her mouth and the rest on her face.

CC had been sitting upright independently and putting items to her mouth with control for a week or two. Her first food explorations with dad were exciting and opened the door for many food adventures. Just before CC turned six months old, Leslie and her husband had discussed the signs for readiness and the safety steps they were going to put in place to support her self-feeding process. And she couldn't even wait for mom to get home from work!

Both of us were excited to start this journey of feasting with our little ones. But before we jumped on the wagon, we too had to get ready for the ride. There are key things to focus on during this time, and there's no need to rush feeding baby table foods. She's got her whole life to eat. Let's make sure she's ready.

The *Born To Eat* Approach Can Look Different for Everyone

Keep in mind that if your infant was born early, or was premature, he may need more time to catch up on growth and development prior to starting solids. For example, if baby was born at thirty-two weeks (instead of forty), he *may* need about eight more weeks to catch up developmentally. Some children who are born early, or that have special health care needs, may have low muscle tone and need a little extra help with the process. This could look like a combination of self-feeding and spoon-feeding along with some gentle support in sitting. Children who have higher energy demands, like those with some lung and heart conditions, may need to have a focus on higher-energy foods and formulas. Some children may have issues with feeding right away and may have oral aversions related to feeding or medical traumas. This could lead to significant feeding difficulties and or the use of a feeding tube.

An incredible group of feeding professionals believe kids with special health care needs can still self-regulate and listen to their bodies. They, and their parents, just need the right support and tools to engage in a *child-centered* feeding therapy program (that can also guide in other therapeutic measures based on the child's needs). With support of feeding specialists–like many speech language pathologists, occupational therapists, physical therapists, pediatricians, and registered dietitians–a child with special health needs can also embrace the *Born to Eat* approach. It may just look different–and that's okay.

Although the American Academy of Pediatrics once recommended the introduction of solid foods beginning at four months of age, they have since updated the recommendation to a more physically and developmentally appropriate six months old. Six months is not a magical age; however, it's a great guide. Parents must consider baby's gastrointestinal system, physical development, dexterity, and oral readiness when starting solid foods.

We feel that baby should be at or around six months of age and developmentally appropriate to start solid foods. It's important to note that biological age and developmental age are not the same thing. Every baby progresses at their own pace. And, regardless of whether your child is breastfed, formula fed, or a combination of both, around six months is the general recommendation for adding complementary foods.[1] Ultimately, it's up to you and your physician to determine whether your little one is developmentally ready to start table foods. Developmental signs of readiness would include, but aren't limited to, sitting unassisted, absence of tongue thrust, grasping items with more hand control, and putting toys to his or her mouth.

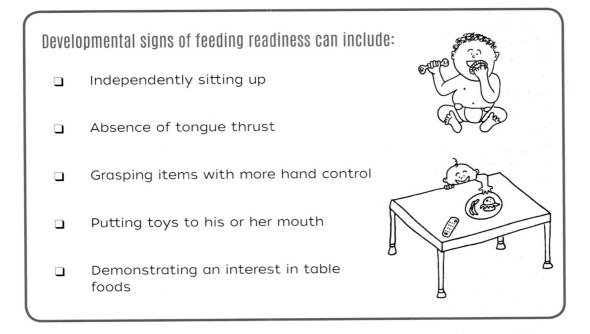

Developmental signs of feeding readiness can include:

- ❏ Independently sitting up

- ❏ Absence of tongue thrust

- ❏ Grasping items with more hand control

- ❏ Putting toys to his or her mouth

- ❏ Demonstrating an interest in table foods

Not only do we have to look at baby's readiness, but we must also examine our own. This is the time to evaluate the family's food and eating patterns along with potential risks. Eating is a family affair. If the family's primary intake lacks variety, iron-rich foods, or meal structure, it may be time to explore new recipes and grocery items. If family meals happen in front of a favorite television show, it's most definitely time to move it to the table. This isn't just for a family meal experience and increased mindfulness; it's also for baby's safety.

Is Baby Ready?

Baby Jill was six months old. She'd been sitting upright for a week or two and her parents were eager to start her on solids. Jill had been watching mom and dad eat for weeks. While she was playing with toys, she dropped them often and did not move them toward her mouth.

❑   Ready

✔   Not Ready, Baby Jill is not that interested in food just yet. She must first shows signs of mouthing objects or reaching for foods. Hold off introducing foods so frustration is avoided.

Baby Alex was almost six months old. He'd been chewing his favorite block toys and handing them to mom and dad. At dinnertime, he'd sit in his high chair and play while mom and dad ate. He kept reaching for their food.

✔   Ready, Baby Alex is showing signs of readiness to try eating. Sit him down for his first meal.

❑   Not Ready

If you and baby are ready, securely fasten her into a high chair and start with foods finger-sized and -shaped. Remember, baby's sole nutrition source is still breast milk or infant formula during this time. It's about skill-building with the bonus of some added nutrition, which is why we call this stage the pre-feeding beginner. Baby needs to hold the food, explore the texture in her hands, and get used to how it feels in her mouth. Our first foods included bananas, ripe or cooked pears, steamed sweet potatoes, scrambled eggs, avocados, and sliced steak. These are the foods we eat, and so the family meal begins. But first, let's make sure we're off to a safe start. A randomized controlled trial (one of the best types of studies) in New Zealand, called *Baby-Led Introduction to Solids Study (BLISS)*, provided safety points to participants using this feeding method with their infants.[2] The BLISS protocol was designed as a modified version of BLW that addresses the common concerns of choking risk, potential for low iron intake, and poor growth due to a possibility of lower energy intakes by parental

education. As nutrition professionals, we had these items in mind as we practiced the approach with our own children and found the educational tips and advice in the BLISS protocol very useful. We realized that our methods for keeping baby safe were right on track with their study protocol, so we've combined them here.

Pre-Feeding Beginner Safety List

1. Secure baby upright in a high chair or feeding seat. Baby should never be reclined or eating in someone's lap. As tempting as it is to hold that sweet baby in your lap, don't do it. Sitting in a high chair allows the parent or caregiver to evaluate how baby is doing at all times and respond to their cues.

2. **Never** leave baby alone when eating.

3. Let baby put food in his mouth. He needs to be in control of how fast the food enters his mouth or how much he eats at all times. As tempting as it is, you don't have to help.

4. If the food has been cooked, test the temperature of the food to ensure it has cooled enough for baby to test. Even something perceived as warm by the caregiver may be felt as hot by a baby. Lukewarm is a good introductory temperature. There's no need to have everything cold, and it is best to introduce a variety of temperatures at each meal.

5. Test the texture of the food by mashing between your fingers gently or pressing between your lips to make sure the food can be mashed with baby's gums. If not, it's not the right texture. Consider cooking the food longer or picking a different food.

6. Offer foods that have been cut or are in the form of a finger so baby can pick it up. This should a bit longer than baby's fist (like baby's fist and a half for gripping).

7. Don't offer foods that easily break off into small pieces or crumbs that could potentially block the airway of baby, as they can pose a choking risk. Foods we recommend avoiding at *this stage* due to increased risk of choking include raw apples, whole grapes, whole cherry tomatoes, other raw fruits or vegetables with tough skins, nuts, thick nut-butters, popcorn, marshmallows, hard candy, hot dogs, very crusty bread, or any food in a round or coin-like shape.

Talking Texture with Feeding Expert and Pediatric Speech Therapist Jacqueline P. Henry, MA, SLP, CCC

Food comes in many different textures. You have probably heard the most about food textures in relation to baby food stages, usually beginning with smooth purées then transitioning to a chunkier purée. Many use baby cereal at this point. Next, melt-able solids like puffs or soft crackers are introduced. Purées are often presented via a spoon with an adult setting pace and size of bites. Melt-able solids allow for self-feeding. The last stage of most baby foods, which often contain chunks in a variety of textures, are where many kiddos begin to show difficulty managing and/or tolerating new textures. This can lead to meal-related stress for kids and anxiety for the parents, thus ending up in need of feeding therapy. Of course, many children do fine from beginning to end of the popular progression promoted so heavily in our society, but for some, it's the perfect storm.

After reviewing this progression of texture introduction with parents, I switch it up and dive into self-feeding as a more efficient alternative. Keep in mind, I work with children who have delayed or disordered eating and need intervention, but I used BLW with my daughter and the results were so positive that I tossed the BLW components into my therapy toolbox. The benefits, in my opinion, are twofold. First, self-feeding builds confidence and promotes fine motor skills to get the food from plate to mouth. Second, exposure to food shapes and textures in a setting where the kiddo has control promotes a higher frequency of attempts and enjoyment. Imagine, as an adult, you had to attempt to do something you have never done before. There are two scenarios. In the first, you are in control of your learning and attempts to complete the task. In the second, someone is standing over you directing your every move, possibly even grabbing your hands and giving (unsolicited) hand-over-hand assistance. My blood pressure is inching upward just imagining it! In the second situation, I doubt you would learn the skill, but instead attach a stress reaction to the memory. As a child mouths toys, they are preparing their mouth for a wide range of food shapes and textures. In BLW, food is used in the same way. We aren't expecting a six-month-old to gain adequate nutrition from self-feeding, but as a way to sharpen food management skills. When mouthing food, the tongue darts around, chasing the food. Just like when you have something stuck in your teeth. Your tongue just can't stay away! Eventually, through self-feeding practice, the child will develop the side-to-side tongue movement needed to manage a piece of food while chewing. Really, it all comes down to giving you baby control and experience. Happy eating!

Priority Nutrients

One of the main concerns about starting solids or complementary foods is getting certain nutrients that *may* be at lower levels now in baby's body. At the time of our writing, no research has been done to determine if babies following a baby-led weaning approach have any greater risk of iron deficiency than traditionally-fed infants.[3] Regardless of the feeding approach, iron is a top-priority nutrient when starting solid foods. Before you pop open a box of iron-fortified infant cereal, let's start with the 4-1-1 on iron. Iron carries oxygen throughout our bodies. If you consider what's happening the first year of a baby's life, particularly in brain development, you recognize the importance of oxygen getting to the brain.

In short, if a body does not have enough iron, oxygen struggles to move around the body, which is of particular importance to brain development and baby's immune system. Iron deficiency can cause anemia, which can lead to fatigue, growth, and learning issues.[4] We all need iron, but our babies, in a stage of crucial growth and development, absolutely need iron. Identifying iron deficiency anemia in infants can be challenging. It's best to beef up their iron intake from the start, literally. Long before fortified baby foods, most babies thrived on whole food sources of iron. Once upon a time, meats were considered hard for babies to digest and many thought an early introduction of meat may put them at risk for allergies and possibly even kidney distress. We realize now that this was not and is not the case. Meats are our first foods.

Leslie still remembers when Dr. Julie told her that the newest recommendation was to start with meats and iron-rich foods. She was so happy to hear her doctor say those words (because that was her plan anyway). We now know that iron-rich foods should be introduced to babies early on when they're developmentally ready and starting solids. While starting the process, baby still depends on milk feedings as a primary energy source. Both formula and breast milk provide some iron. Fortified infant formula has (what appears to be) ample iron at 10 to 13 milligrams (mg) per liter, yet the bioavailability, or how much the body can actually breakdown and utilize, of the iron is only around 4 percent.[5] Breast milk is thought to be very low in iron yet it has a very high bioavailability of approximately 50 percent.[6] So generally speaking, breast milk and formula may deliver about the same amount of iron based on bioavailability. Now, in the second part of infancy, baby just needs more iron.

The Recommended Daily Allowance (RDA) of iron for an infant seven to twelve months old is approximately 11 mg (only 0.7 mg absorbed) per day due to rapid growth within the first year of life. Now, if you want to use some infant cereal, you can, but there are ample ways your baby can get whole-food iron sources without it. Although infant cereals have a high amount of iron per serving (18 mg) the actual bioavailability is roughly 3 percent, whereas the bioavailability of animal sources of iron is around 15.5 percent.[7] These whole-food sources of iron, coupled with a food high in vitamin C, or ascorbic acid, to increase the absorption of iron in baby's body can help baby get the iron he needs.

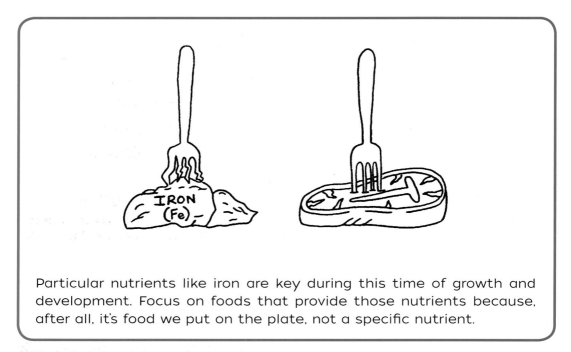

Particular nutrients like iron are key during this time of growth and development. Focus on foods that provide those nutrients because, after all, it's food we put on the plate, not a specific nutrient.

It's possible you're still wondering—must baby get iron only from fortified cereals? Whole foods have been around a lot longer with greater bioavailability, so our opinion is no. We're not saying you can't use it. We're just saying you shouldn't feel like it's a requirement that you use fortified cereals. Fortified cereals also only provide about ten calories per tablespoon so that's not a lot of energy for baby. Neither of us used infant cereals and our little ones' iron levels were just fine. We feel that if you're offering quality whole-food sources that are iron-rich, you're on the right path. Here are a few examples of high-bioavailable food sources. Most animal sources of iron have higher bioavailability, yet many plant sources offer some iron benefits, as well.

Heme Iron Sources (Animal Sources)		
Food	*Baby-Sized Portion*	*Iron Content*
Egg, hard boiled	½ large	0.3 milligrams
Beef, Ground (85% lean)	1-ounce	0.83 milligrams
Beef Steak, Top Sirloin	1-ounce	0.97 milligrams
Beef Liver, pan fried	1-ounce	1.7 milligrams
Chicken Liver, braised	1-ounce	3.3 milligrams
Non-Heme Iron Sources (Plant-based)		
Food	*Baby-Sized Portion*	*Iron Content*
Black Beans	1 Tablespoon	0.28 milligrams
Lentils	1 Tablespoon	0.4 milligrams
MaltOMeal, made with water	1 Tablespoon	1.1 milligrams
Chocolate, Dark, 70-85%	0.5-ounce	1.69 milligrams

US Department of Agriculture, Agricultural Research Service. USDA National Nutrient Database for Standard Reference, Release 26 external link disclaimer. Nutrient Data Laboratory Home Page, 2013. (https://ndb.nal.usda.gov// Accessed on 09/13/2016)

Foods to Start With

We don't want you to get all caught up on the numbers. That's a recipe that can really get us stressed out—parents don't need any more of that. Instead, let's focus on getting in iron-rich foods at most meals and, when you can, pair it with foods that are a source of vitamin C, which is known to increase the absorption of the iron. Once we're just starting to feed our little one solids, we'll stick with individual foods on the plate so we can monitor their progress. We'll move on to the family's favorite mixed meals at around seven to eight months of age. For now, these are foods we recommend starting with and then we'll build from there. The BLISS Protocol suggests to build a meal in this fashion. Pick an iron-rich food, add a high-energy food, and also a fruit and/or vegetable side.[8] We feel that this template makes it much easier to build baby's plate to get the necessary starter foods.

Sample Vitamin C Sources

Kiwi	Tomatoes
Orange	Pineapple
Red bell pepper	Mango
Papaya	Broccoli
Strawberries	Cauliflower
Raspberries	

We've got those iron-rich foods down now, so let's talk about high-energy foods and fruits and veggies. High-energy foods are just that—foods that are calorically dense. Baby is growing at a tremendous rate, and when offering first foods, we want them to get as much energy and nutrition as they can in every little bite. We used high-energy foods like avocadoes, meats, regular (not low-fat) Greek yogurt, cheese, butter/oil for seasoning, runny nut butters, and eggs. These high-energy foods typically have higher amounts of fat, which are crucial for brain development, growth, and self-regulation. You'll also note that some of the foods overlap categories, like regular Greek yogurt is great for protein and provides high-energy. Avocado is a tasty, satisfying fruit, but we put it in the high-energy category because of the energy it provides as a super healthy fat source. Just pick a spot for it on the plate and fill in the rest.

Next up on baby's plate is the fruit and/or vegetable side. As we mentioned, those higher in vitamin C are a good choice when serving up the iron-rich foods, but you don't have to do that at every meal. Baby can get lots of variety and introductions to food by offering a wide selection of fruits and veggies prepared in different ways. We've created this list for you so that, early on in the feeding process, all you have to do is pick one from each column to build your meal. This isn't a complete list. You'll add to this list with your own family foods, but we hope this will set you up for a great start. As you and baby gain more confidence with feeding, it'll become second nature.

Pick a Food from Each Column and Build Baby's Meal
*Iron-rich food **Vitamin C source

Protein Foods	High-Energy Foods	Fruit/Vegetable Sides
*Beef, sirloin, flank, flatiron, roast, finger-sliced	Avocado, ripe, sliced	Carrots, shredded or thin sticks, soft steamed
*Beef, ground, soft cooked or rolled into finger-like sticks then cooked	Soft/runny nut butters (natural peanut or almond)	Banana, very ripe, cut in half

| Pick a Food from Each Column and Build Baby's Meal |||
| *Iron-rich food **Vitamin C source |||
Protein Foods	**High-Energy Foods**	**Fruit/Vegetable Sides**
*Eggs, scrambled or hard-boiled, cut into slices	Whole fat, unflavored Greek yogurt	Pears, ripe and soft, thinly sliced
*Chicken, soft, white or dark meat, finger-sliced or ground	Extra virgin olive oil	**Sweet potatoes, steamed or baked without skin
Fatty fish (salmon or trout fillets, skinless), small chunks	Chia seeds (or chia pudding)	Green beans, soft, boiled or steamed
*Tuna, canned chunk light, small chunks	Chocolate, dark 65% plus, broken into grippable pieces	*Lentils, cooked in chicken stock and canned tomatoes
*Pork, chops, tender-loin, or roast, tender and finger-sliced	Soft buttered toast, finger-sliced, or soft crackers, like grahams	*Beans, extra soft/smashable black, kidney, or pinto beans
*Turkey, soft, white or dark meat, finger-sliced	Olives, chopped	**Strawberries, sliced, soft fresh or frozen and defrosted (great texture at this stage)
*Turkey, ground, soft cooked or rolled into fin-ger-like sticks then cooked	Coconut milk (good for cooking with, not drink-ing as babies drink breast milk or formula)	**Raspberries, halved
*Game meat (venison, duck, rabbit, or elk)	Cheese, shredded or grated	**Tomatoes, thinly sliced
*Lamb, sliced or ground, soft cooked or rolled into finger-like sticks then cooked	Whole-fat cottage or ricotta cheese	**Kiwi, very ripe and core removed, sliced
*Beans (lentils or extra soft/smashable black, kid-ney, or pinto beans)		**Broccoli, raw or soft-steamed, stem with flower top for ease of holding

Pick a Food from Each Column and Build Baby's Meal		
*Iron-rich food **Vitamin C source		
Protein Foods	**High-Energy Foods**	**Fruit/Vegetable Sides**
		**Orange, de-segmented without any inner skins at first

Just like when we work with clients and ask them to visualize a plate to balance it, we can do the same for our little one's meals. This *fill in the plate* method of building baby's meal makes it much easier to put a balanced meal on the table. Pick one from the protein-rich foods, the high-energy foods, and fruit/vegetable side and just *fill in the plate*. Don't forget, we have our first foods recipes for you to try in chapter 14.

Here are some quick meal ideas that pair high-iron foods with high–vitamin C foods:

½ Boiled Egg
3 Raspberries
2 Soft Steamed
    Green Beans

2 Tbsp. Lentils
2 Frozen Strawberries
1 Raw Broccoli Stalk
    and Floret

1 oz. Sirloin Steak
1 Kiwi Wedge
1 Sweet Potato Finger

> If the food is slippery, try rolling it in almond meal (finely ground almond flour) or ground oatmeal so baby can get a good grip.

Miss A was not interested in playing with her food. Nope, this girl dove right in and insisted on chewing to swallow. Wendy Jo kicked off her daughter's eating adventures with boiled sweet potato wedges, a juicy wedge of steak, and avocado slices. Let's just say steak was the winner, not only for Miss A, but for mama's confidence, too. Miss A sucked out every drop of juice from that steak finger and even sucked on a second piece before they got chucked overboard to her pups. With meals, Wendy Jo had to ensure that the foods were a safe texture, because Miss A was going to find a way to swallow her food. After a couple weeks of meals, and a couple meal meltdowns had occurred in which Miss A wasn't getting in the food fast enough and was turning hangry (our favorite term for being hungry and angry), Wendy Jo realized she needed to breastfeed Miss A before her meals. This way, Miss A wasn't overly hungry and had more patience for learning to deal with the food. And then learning process begins. We can look back and see clearly that Miss A was *Born to Eat.*

> Cooking influences the amount of iron lost in juices; therefore, it's hard to estimate the amount of iron lost. Research suggests that juices from the meat provide a source of iron.[9] Our little eaters can get the nutrient-rich benefit.

This may not be everyone's experience. Many babies may just play with their foods—smash it, roll it, toss it, or gnaw on it before they ever show interest in actually eating or swallowing the foods. There can be a variety of reasons this happens. The important thing to know is that all babies are different, and they will advance when they are ready. Avoid assuming a baby dislikes a food because they don't eat it; instead, recognize this is part of their learning process. Keep trying foods without expectations. Likes and dislikes come much later in a child's development. At this stage, all foods are fair game (unless there's a known allergy).

> Offer milk feedings prior to meals at the beginning. This way, baby isn't too hungry to skill build and doesn't move too fast with new foods and textures.

The Role of the Spoon

At first, if all baby does is gnaw on the spoon throughout the meal, that's okay! This is the time for learning. Nourishment comes soon. Little ones can use a helping hand; you can show them how to guide the spoon effectively to their mouths before food is even on it. The spoon can be used as a chewing toy, a tool for learning, and a mode of feeding. Parents can mimic how a spoon is used during playtime and mealtime, then reinforce spoon use by placing a loaded spoon on the high chair tray when it's time to start feeding. Helping little ones who are learning to self-feed by putting foods like yogurt, applesauce, ground meats, and other mashed foods on the spoon is an excellent way to get a beginner eater comfortable with spoons. Once your little one begins to toddle around, avoid letting them walk with a spoon in their mouth, as tripping and falling are frequent with new walkers.

Mealtimes may be better earlier for some or later for others. Choose what time of day your baby can have the most success. You may not be putting three meals on the table per day at first, so don't worry. Let your baby (and your intuition) guide you.

Caution Foods

There are foods that we suggest avoiding at least initially, like we mentioned earlier in our pre-feeding beginner safety checklist. These are foods that a baby's gums can break off in large chunks, but cannot chew before they swallow (e.g., raw apple, raw carrot, raw

Did You Know?

While your little one is beginning to explore foods, tastes, and textures, he's learning, as well. Let's break down some of the developmental skills baby is honing in on while eating. We'll start with the palmer and pincer (not pincher). A baby is born with the innate ability to grasp objects. By three months, he'll begin to work on this skill and will make significant progress as each month passes. Around four to seven months old, a baby will pick up larger foods, like carrots and broccoli, with an immature palmar grasp and draw them to her mouth.

She will likely be able to grasp smaller foods such as peas and blueberries by raking it toward her with her hand and squeezing it into her fist. Don't expect a precise grasp just yet. At around eight to twelve months, baby will start picking up those blueberries with a more refined pincer grasp using her thumb and forefinger.

celery, round foods, crumb-like foods). In chapter 14, we have an extensive list of foods that can pose choking risks and how to best modify or avoid these foods. Bigger pieces of food that break off into their mouth can pose a risk until a baby is ready to chew and swallow or chew and spit. Gagging is normal and part of the learning process. Once they learn how to handle a gag, babies then continue to learn which foods are easier for them to chew (or not chew) and will often spit out foods that they are not ready to swallow. This takes time to identify and can be different from infant to infant, so take your time and watch for those cues. We felt confident with these starter foods right away.

Born to Eat Starter Foods

1. Avocado, ¼ to ⅛ of an avocado sliced lengthwise.
2. Steamed carrots or sweet potatoes, 1-inch slices steamed to a very soft texture or mashed.
3. Beef, medium to medium-well steak slices, about baby's fist and a half in length.
4. Whole fat Greek yogurt plain or with ½ teaspoon of nut butter swirled into 2 to 3 tablespoons of yogurt. This gets messy, but it's a great way to introduce nuts safely and a source of probiotics for baby. We'll touch more on probiotics in chapter 9.
5. Eggs, boiled or scrambled. Served boiled eggs thinly sliced, just the yolk, or mashed like egg salad.
6. Soft fruits like pears and kiwi sliced into strips.
7. High-allergen foods like eggs, nut butters, shrimp, and dairy products. Shrimp is slippery and can be tough to gnaw. We like to grind it at first and serve like a shrimp salad. *Remember to discuss this progression with baby's pediatrician if you feel there's an allergy risk. Nut butters need to be added to yogurt or a thin layer on a soft piece of toast.*
8. Raw and steamed broccoli, stalk and floret, so baby can hold on to the stalk. When serving raw, remove any small pieces baby breaks off. Baby may successfully get off tiny, individual flower buds. Important side note on raw broccoli— raw broccoli is a choking risk. Before our babies could successfully bite off any piece of the broccoli, we let them teethe on the raw broccoli stalk floret. They were able to gnaw off the tiny, individual flower buds and get the flavor of raw broccoli, but not able to bite off a piece. We also served steamed florets and removed the stalk from the table once the *tree* portion was gone. Go with your comfort level and what your baby's gnawing skills are at the start. If any teeth are present, we suggest steamed and very soft broccoli.

> ## Wait until One Year for These Foods
>
> Drinking Cow's Milk—Because baby should be consuming breast milk or infant formula. Other dairy forms are fine.
>
> Honey—Due to risk of the toxin *Clostridium botulinum*, which can be very serious for an infant's gastrointestinal system.
>
> Lunch Meats and Fresh Cheeses like goat and feta—Due the possibility of the possible growth of *Listeria monocytogenes* leading to listeriosis. Listeria can grow in refrigerator-like temperatures.

Just One Food at a Time? Not Necessarily.

There are families out there with infants who are at higher risk for food allergies. With this in mind, some recommendations for introducing foods included starting with one food per three to seven days and then trying a new food in the following days. We have friends and professional colleagues in this boat, and they have chosen to give it a little more time between introductions. That is perfectly fine! Chat with your pediatrician if you're concerned about a food allergy and make that choice together.

> Emerging research suggests that giving high-allergen foods as soon as a child is developmentally appropriate to consume solids may reduce the risk of the development of some food allergies, particularly egg and peanut.[10]

If you don't have a family history of food allergies, there's no evidence to date that suggests a one food at a time approach prevents the development of an allergy. We introduced our little ones to what we ate from day one. We didn't do the one food per three to seven days progression, but some do—you're the parent, you choose what's right for you and your baby. We felt that introducing food variety in the same amount of our own family variety was beneficial. Research suggests introducing as many flavors and textures to babies as often as possible may increase the overall acceptance of foods later on in life. For example, folks in India make curry dishes. You won't find a curried chicken on a kids menu in the United States, yet babies in India eat curry all the time. It's all about exposure and family culture. It's up to you.

The 4-1-1 on Seafood and Babies

Eat fish, don't eat fish, eat fish but not raw, eat fish but not those high in mercury—it's hard to know what to do! The message frequently changes, but that's a good thing. It means research is evolving, diving into the deep sea for answers. At the time of our writing, seafood is a go with babies. There are some fish to avoid, such as tilefish, monkfish, shark, and swordfish. These dirty four are known to have high levels of mercury. As for tuna, look for the can that says chunk light versus albacore tuna. Albacore has 40 micrograms of mercury per 4 ounces, whereas chunk light tuna only has 13 micrograms. According to the Food and Drug Administration (FDA) official website, it's considered safe to provide two to three servings of seafood in age-appropriate portions each week.[10] The *Born to Eat* team both kicked off with chunk light tuna in the first month of eating; see our recipe for tuna salad in chapter 16.

Is Baby Eating Enough?

At this stage in the game, your baby is taking in formula or breast milk as their primary nutrition, so everything else is exploratory. They are getting in breast milk or formula that provides ample calories, so relax if they aren't eating much of the solid food that you offer. The truth of the matter is, your baby has their entire life ahead of them to eat. Take this slow. If you need to start with just one meal per day, that's fine.

You choose what you chew, as well as which foods your baby chews, but they choose how much. Remember the Division of Responsibility? This begins at first bite. Although the temptation to say *one more bite* may linger on your tongue and in your mind, let those words stay put. If you find your baby is getting frustrated with every bite, try feeding your baby with breast milk or formula before the meal. Remember—at first, we don't want baby to come to the plate super hungry. Her skills aren't ready to deliver the full nourishment of a meal. The only time Wendy Jo found herself coaching in food has been when Miss A was sick. Wendy Jo realized that she needed a reminder to *chew, chew, chew*. This helped her realize that the lack of appetite was related to Miss A being ill. During this time, she nursed a lot more and hardly ate at mealtimes. If this happens, don't panic. When your little one feels better, you can resume more solid food feedings.

What Is Coaching?

When we use the term *coaching*, we simply mean using supportive words like *chew, chew, chew*, or, as we move forward, the phrase *spit it out*. We use these only for reasons of safety and that's it. We do not recommend comments like *just a little more, keep eating*, or *that's enough*. This can feel like pressure to eat or stop eating and we want baby to lead the way.

Early on, little ones tend to check in more with the pediatrician. At first monthly, and once they hit about six months of age, about every two to three months. If your little one is filling diapers and maintaining their growth curve, it's most likely they're getting enough. We both had great experiences with our pediatrician's offices and knew that if we needed a quick check-in visit for reassurance, that wouldn't be a problem.

Chapter 5 References

1. "Infant Food and Feeding," American Academy of Pediatrics, accessed August 19, 2016, https://www.aap.org/en-us/advocacy-and-policy/aap-health-initia-tives/HALF-Implementation-Guide/Age-Specific-Content/pages/infant-food-and-feeding.aspx

2. Sonya L. Cameron, Anne-Louise M. Heath, Rachael W. Taylor, "How Feasible Is Baby-Led Weaning as an Approach to Infant Feeding? A Review of the Evidence," *Nutrients* 4(11) (2012): 1575–1609, doi:10.3390/nu4111575.

3. Sonya L. Cameron, Anne-Louise M. Heath, Rachael W. Taylor, "How Feasible Is Baby-Led Weaning as an Approach to Infant Feeding? A Review of the Evidence," *Nutrients* 4(11) (2012): 1575–1609, doi:10.3390/nu4111575.

4. Robert D. Baker, Frank R. Greer, The Committee on Nutrition, "From the American Academy of Pediatrics Clinical Report, Diagnosis and Prevention of Iron Deficiency and Iron-Deficiency Anemia in Infants and Young Children (0–3 Years of Age)," *Pediatrics* 126 (5) (November 2010), date accessed October 4, 2016, http://pediatrics.aappublications.org/content/126/5/1040.

5. Lena Davidsson, Peter Kastenmayer, Hanna Szajewska, Richard F. Hurrell, Denis Barclay, "Iron bioavailability in infants from an infant cereal fortified with

ferric pyrophosphate or ferrous fumarate," *American Journal of Clinical Nutrition* 71(6) (June 2000):1597–602, accessed October 4, 2016, http://ajcn.nutrition. org/content/71/6/1597.long.

6. UM Saarinen, MA Siimes, PR Dallman, "Iron absorption in infants: high bio-availability of breast milk iron as indicated by the extrinsic tag method of iron absorption and by the concentration of serum ferritin," *Journal of Pediatrics* 91(1) (July 1977): 36–9, PR. http://www.ncbi.nlm.nih.gov/pubmed/577504

7. Sonya L. Cameron, Anne-Louise M. Heath, Rachael W. Taylor, "How Feasible Is Baby-Led Weaning as an Approach to Infant Feeding? A Review of the Evidence," *Nutrients* 4(11) (2012): 1575–1609, doi:10.3390/nu4111575.

8. Lisa Daniels, Anne-Louise M. Heath, Sheila M. Williams, Sonya L. Cameron, Elizabeth A. Fleming, Barry J. Taylor, Ben J. Wheeler, Rosalind S. Gibson, Rachael W. Taylor, "Baby-Led Introduction to SolidS (BLISS) study: a randomised controlled trial of a baby-led approach to complementary feeding," *BMC Pediatrics* 15 (2015): 179, doi:10.1186/s12887-015-0491-8.

9. Roger Purchas, David Simcock, Trevor Knight, Brian Wilkinson, "Variation in the form of iron in beef and lamb meat and losses of iron during cooking and storage," *International Journal of Food Science & Technology* 38 (2003): 827–837, doi:10.1046/j.1365-2621.2003.00732.x.

10. Despo Ierodiakonou, Vanessa Garcia-Larsen, Andrew Logan, Annabel Groome, Sergio Cunha, Jennifer Chivinge, Zoe Robinson, Natalie Geoghegan, Katharine Jarrold, Tim Reeves, Nara Tagiyeva-Milne, Ulugbek Nurmatov, MD, Marialena Trivella, Jo Leonardi-Bee, Robert J. Boyle, MD, "Timing of Allergenic Food Introduction to the Infant Diet and Risk of Allergic or Autoimmune Disease: A Systematic Review and Meta-analysis," *Journal of American Medical Association* 316(11) (2016): 1181–1192, doi:10.1001/jama.2016.12623.

CHAPTER 6

EXPLORATION
(7 TO 8 MONTHS–THE BEGINNER)

> "Children have never been very good at listening to their elders, but they have never failed to imitate them."
>
> —James Baldwin

Leslie's daughter, CC, loved being including in the family meal. She'd been so excited to try many first foods when she was just over six months old. Now CC was just over seven months and seemed to have a handle on picking up food, and actually eating it! She moved from smashing food with her palm and raking it toward her mouth to a more refined method. She was able to pick up a bean or berry now just with her thumb and forefinger. Leslie and her husband were excited to see her explore so many textures and try so many foods. Now, it was time to step it up a notch for little CC. She liked tomatoes, she loved beef, she could eat loads of beans—it was time to let CC experience

mixed-ingredient meals, like her family's favorite chili. It's still her favorite food to date, even when it's 100 degrees out.

Is Baby Ready?

Baby Ann was grabbing for the foods on mom's plate after she ate her ground beef crumbles, sliced tomatoes, and avocado. She picked up the smaller pieces of her sliced tomato with the tips of her fingers, a much more precise movement than when she started with solids a few weeks before. Now she was sitting with her parents trying to eat at breakfast and dinner.

- ✔ Ready, Baby Ann is showing signs of the pincer grasp and is ready to move forward.
- ❑ Not Ready

Baby Joe was happy to sit at the dinner table with mom and dad for all of his meals. He now consumed most of his meals and demanded to nurse less throughout the day.

- ✔ Ready, Baby Joe is progressing and ready to join in more meals.
- ❑ Not Ready

Baby Evan was really having a lot of fun with his food. He found it interesting to watch most of the food on his plate hit the floor. When he tried to use the side of his hand to rake food toward his mouth, he'd end up smashing more than he got in his mouth. He seemed content just playing with his spoon versus using it to eat food.

- ❑ Ready
- ✔ Not Ready, Baby Evan is still enjoying play with food and this is okay. Continue looking for signs of readiness to move forward with meals.

Is Your Little One Ready to Move On?

Hopefully by now you're feeling like this self-feeding stuff is really great! And it's messy but not that bad. As you're supporting your little one, you've likely noticed some changes in skills and how he's actually eating. It's time to check in and see how your baby is progressing. Is he eating more at each meal? How many meals per day does he enjoy with the family? Is his pincer grasp developing? And what goes in, must come out. Those diapers are likely changing, too. Many babies are just starting to take in enough food to alter their poo color. This is an excellent (and stinky) way to tell how much baby is eating. If baby's poo is still yellow, then it's likely he's still learning and playing with food versus eating most of it. The yellowish color suggests that the diet is still predominantly milk-based. The color turning more toward brown is a good indicator that baby is beginning to eat and digest more whole foods. And it's likely that baby is graduating from a pre-eating beginner to a beginner eater.

Let's take a moment to see how your little one is progressing with feeding skills, texture tolerance, and food intake. Use this checklist to determine if baby is ready to move from pre-feeding beginner to a beginner.

- Eating more, 2 to 3 meals per day
- Grasping items with more palm and finger control
- Able to accept and tolerate a variety of textures (smooth, chewy, soft, lumpy, liquid-y)
- Getting spoon effectively in mouth
- Able to eat most of meal (3 to 6 tablespoons per meal)
- Introduction of a sippy, straw, or open cup (best filled slightly with breast milk or formula at this stage)
- Banging, dropping, throwing, and smashing are fascinating baby at this stage
- Reaching out for more food or eating second helpings of food

If baby doesn't quite have all of these down, that's fine. Give it another week or so and reevaluate. Remember the timeline is one of readiness and skill development, not specific age. Once he's eating more and getting food to his mouth more effectively, we can continue with the *fill the plate* method and begin to add a larger variety of individual and mixed foods. But safety first! Let's review safety for the beginner.

Beginner Self-Feeder Safety Checklist

1. Babies are getting more mobile at this stage, so don't forget to strap them in at the table.
2. **Never** leave a baby unattended while eating. Although you may be gaining more confidence in their feeding capabilities, they can still get tired, relaxed, or overly excited and could take in too much at one time. Babies need to be watched and coached appropriately any time food is present.
3. Test the temperature and texture of the food by mashing between your fingers gently or pressing between your lips to make sure the food can be mashed with baby's gums. If not, it's not the right texture. Consider cooking the food longer or picking a different food.
4. Still offer foods that have been cut or are in the form of a finger so baby can pick them up. This should be about one and half times as long as baby's fist.
5. Don't offer foods that easily break off into small pieces or crumbs that could potentially block baby's airway, as they can pose a choking risk. Foods we recommend avoiding at this stage due to increased risk of choking include raw apples, whole grapes, whole cherry tomatoes, nuts, thick nut-butters, popcorn, marshmallows, hard candy, hot dogs, very hard crusty bread, or any food in a round or coin-like shape.
6. If baby manages to break off small pieces of a harder food, remove from table. Do not remove food from baby's mouth. Coach baby to spit out any foods that are unsafe. Then remove food from table.
7. If your baby has teeth at this stage, it may be best to avoid raw foods that can break off easily (such as carrots, celery, apple, and broccoli). Their teeth may allow them to bite off more than they can chew, literally. These can be served cooked, and raw can be reintroduced when your baby shows signs of being skilled in chewing or spitting out foods they cannot swallow safely.

Priority Nutrients

With one month into the adventures of eating, there's a good chance your little one is still not eating all that much, perhaps only one quarter cup to one cup per day. Babies vary in intake, so don't fret if breast milk or infant formulas are still their main source of nutrition. This is normal and is the recommendation through one year of age. As previously mentioned, iron is an important nutrient to focus on, and that continues throughout the first year (and throughout childhood). Feel free to visit chapter 5 from time to time if you need an iron-rich foods refresher. As we move on with the beginner eater, we'll focus on other important nutrients and foods that are excellent additions at the family dinner table and for baby's growth and development. We'll continue to focus on protein- and iron-rich foods on the plate and add foods that are sources of omega-3 fatty acids, vitamin D, zinc, and probiotics.

OMEGA-3 FATTY ACIDS

It's likely you're familiar with omega-3 fatty acids like docosahexaenoic acid, which is usually referred to as DHA. They're commonly found in prenatal vitamins and added to many products for growing infants and children. The thing to remember about omega-3 fats is that they are *essential* fatty acids. This means that your body cannot make them and they must be ingested through the diet. Omega-3 fatty acids, particularly DHA, is a primary fat found in the brain and essential for central nervous system and retinal development. There are actually three types of omega-3 fatty acids: ALA (alpha-linolenic acid), DHA (docosahexaenoic acid), and EPA (eicosapentaenoic acid). While all are important in a healthy diet, we're focusing primarily on DHA and its crucial role in the body of a developing infant and child. Researchers and food manufacturers alike have realized the importance of these fats across the lifespan. We are now even seeing omega-3 fats as an added component to foods that do not have them naturally. This is called a functional food, and we feel that it's a great and useful advance in food technology and manufacturing. It's a particularly helpful way to get in some nutrients that might not be accessible or readily available for some families or regions. We like to call it whole-food plus.

We suggest incorporating at least one food source of omega-3 fatty acids daily (and not just for baby).

Sources of Omega-3 Fatty Acids

*Salmon   *Crab
*Trout   Edamame
*Sardines   Flaxseed Oil
*Anchovies   *Omega-3 Enriched Eggs
*Herring   Walnuts
*Canned Chunk-Light Tuna   Chia Seeds
*Shrimp

*Sources of DHA

Vitamin D

In recent years, vitamin D, also known as the sunshine vitamin, has gotten plenty of press. It's related to numerous processes in the body beyond bone health, and many Americans have insufficient, if not deficient, levels. While the best source or way to convert vitamin D in the skin to its active and useful form is exposure to sunlight, too much time in the sun can be damaging to the skin. The *Born to Eat* team loves getting our vitamin D from the sunshine. However, we do know that a little can go a long way to provide vitamin D and can quickly turn into too much sun. Many children's and medical organizations recommend sunscreen for most all sun exposure. This is great for keeping that beautiful baby skin but not so good for vitamin D levels.

Low vitamin D is becoming an issue across the lifespan, yet this is of primary concern for breastfed infants and partially-breastfed infants since breast milk has low levels of vitamin D. Currently, the AAP recommends that all infants and children have a minimum intake of 400 IU (International Units) of vitamin D per day. This could be achieved by supplementation of vitamin D for babies who are breastfed or through fortified formula during infancy. It's very unlikely that an infant or child would reach the minimum intake level with food alone. There's a reason they call it the sunshine vitamin and not the fortified food vitamin.

While there are a few food sources that could provide 400 IU of vitamin D, an infant wouldn't consume the serving amount to get the needed vitamin amount. And, some sources, like swordfish, aren't recommended for infants due to high mercury levels. Sockeye salmon provides those great omega fats along with over 400 IU vitamin D per 3 ounces. Baby isn't likely to eat 3 ounces, but it's a solid start and a nutrient-dense food selection for baby's plate.

Sun exposure remains the best way to get this crucial vitamin. Because of this, recommendations are changing around the world and may include more sun exposure. Be sure to check with your pediatrician for the newest information on vitamin D.

Zinc

With foods like beef, poultry, dairy, eggs, nuts, beans, and shellfish landing on baby's plate, he'll be getting sources of zinc, as well. Zinc is an important mineral that aids in immune function and growth and development. It's hard to protect a baby from colds and illness, but we can support his immune system by making sure we're getting food sources of zinc on his plate. The good thing is that many food sources of zinc are also sources of iron, so you don't have to carry around a big list of foods and nutrients.

Probiotics

Along with omega-3s and vitamin D, probiotics are also popular in the media and with food marketers. There's also a focus on probiotics in emerging research. From helping a colicky baby and treatment of eczema to prevention of allergies, probiotics have gained ample attention for their role in infant nutrition.[1] Probiotics are the healthy gut microbes, or bacteria, that aid in digestion and have numerous protective attributes within the human body. Probiotics within the intestines are so important that the gut is often called the second brain, meaning our neurological and physical health are directly connected and benefited by the health of our gut. Research has also suggested that infants who are introduced to family foods earlier, instead of processed foods, have been found to have higher counts of gut bacteria.[2] Although probiotics are shown to be beneficial, the research is still unclear which bacteria are most beneficial for particular ailments. The *Born to Eat* team feels it's best to get in a variety of bacteria from foods. Probiotics are found in fermented foods such as sauerkraut (German cabbage salad), cheese, yogurts, kefir (similar to a yogurt drink, but more probiotics), kimchi (Korean cabbage salad), sourdough breads, and miso (fermented soy paste). Mothers who breastfeed can pass probiotics onto their infants through breast milk, as well as prebiotics, which are the foods that feed probiotics.

Probiotics are beneficial for the entire family, not just your *Born to Eat* baby. If eating fermented foods is a challenge within your home, consider opting for a supplement. If you decide to use a probiotic supplement, select one found in the refrigerator section of your health food store, has at least 10 billion bacteria per serving, and contains at least 4 or more bacterial strains. Talk to your family physician or registered dietitian for help selecting a particular brand or strains. If your baby needs to be on antibiotics for any reason, it's not a bad idea to speak to your physician about using a probiotic supplement following the course of the medicine. Antibiotics kill not only bad bacteria, but also the good. It's imperative to restore the healthy gut microflora once your infant has had their final dose of antibiotics. In addition to lots of Greek yogurt, CC likes her chewable daily probiotic and asks for her *pro-body-otic* every morning.

Adding More Foods, Textures, and Meals

Now you know even more about priority nutrients. These nutrients aren't just important for infants, but they're smart nutrients for the whole family. We've given you lists of foods with varying nutritional properties, and it's important to remember that we don't just eat nutrients, we eat food. With the suggestions we've provided about the nutrients, we can plan some tasty and balanced meals. Not every meal will be perfectly balanced and that's okay (and normal), but it's good to know where to aim. The foods can be added to family meals or incorporated into your family's favorite recipes. This isn't just the time to feed baby well; it's an opportunity to improve nutrition, variety, and food enjoyment for the whole family.

Early on in the feeding process, Leslie remembers being told to avoid spicy foods and flavors with her little one. While she wasn't going to feed CC a habanero pepper straight from the garden, she added jalapeños to her pot of chili and enchilada bake just like always. Leslie didn't (and still doesn't) believe that having a baby meant the whole family had to eat boring, bland food. Just like with every child (and adult), it was important for CC to experience a variety of flavors and decide for herself whether a food was too spicy or just right. Like we mentioned, that same chili is still CC's favorite food, jalapeños, chili powder, and all. On the flip side, it's totally fine to offer a not-so-spicy option, as well. Some parents (and babies) may have issues with reflux and spice may not be the best addition. Not everyone prefers a spicy kick and that's okay!

We feel that variety is actually the true spice of life and how much variety you introduce to your little one is up to you. Just like what you chew is up to you, how you season and spice is up to you, as well. If you can tell your little one is getting a handle on this eating stuff, the family's favorite mixed foods are fair game. Whether you're having lasagna, tacos, burgers, or going out for Thai food, your little one may be ready to be adventurous in his eating, too. Exposure to new foods is key to a more advanced and accepting palate in the years to come. You can break down your dinner for baby in a baby-friendly fashion. Like CC's chili, at first Leslie served it separated on the plate into beans, beef, tomatoes, and shredded cheese.

Don't worry if baby seems turned off by some of the foods offered; they are still exploring and trying to mentally process their experiences. It's a common misinterpretation that while feeding babies, their facial responses are indicative of them liking or disliking a food. At this stage, it's still about discovery, and they're figuring out what a food tastes like, feels like, smells like, crunches, squashes, and smears like—they are not yet deciding whether or not they like or dislike foods. When at all possible, it's best to avoid a reaction of negativity. We still have to watch our facial expressions at times. We all know the concerned scowl look that accompanies the leading question, *Oh, you don't like it?* We have to coach ourselves as parents and others involved in the family meal to avoid phrases like, *Oh, he doesn't like it* or *He hates it.*

This is the time to stay positive and curious with our own reactions while eating and with baby's experience. If you'd like, you can even dial up the reaction of how much you enjoy each bite saying *Yummy, this is so good!* For those of us who truly have negative preference for say, broccoli, this is possibly the time to try it again, or at the very least don't say anything negative about it when it's on our plates. It's important that baby see similar foods on our plates. We're modeling variety, adventure, and trust with our food. If mom or dad doesn't put broccoli on their plate and show baby how to eat and enjoy it, why would baby want to try it? Our babies are watching and learning. Babies and children alike learn by what foods are provided for them to eat and explore. Parents and caregivers then model how it's eaten and enjoyed.

As we're exploring more foods, it may be tempting to offer baby a bite, but remember it's best that they self-feed and self-regulate. If baby reaches for food on another's plate, place a safe piece of that food or offering on their plate, and let them explore. If the family meal happens to be something extremely spicy, remember that babies can be more sensitive to it, so watch them closely for any flushing or an immediate need for breast milk, formula, or water after a spicy bite. Some babies like spicy food, so it's okay to introduce them to these foods as we mentioned with CC's chili. Just stay alert; you will surely find out whether your little one can take the heat. Keep a non-spicy alterative on the back burner just in case.

Did You Know?

Exposure to new foods are key to a more advanced and accepting palate in the years to come. It can take ten, twenty, or *even more* introductions of a food before it's accepted. That goes for both the little ones and big ones in the family. We all have different temperaments that can impact our eating and acceptance of foods. Sometimes it's easy, and sometimes it's not. Just don't give up!

Our Favorite Beginner Mixed Food Meals

It's time introduce some of your favorite family meals. Those meals don't have to be your holiday best recipes; they can just be simple and tasty. Some of our favorite beginner entrées were chicken pot pie, avocado chicken salad, chili, spaghetti and meatballs, chicken curry, shredded pork roast, and a simple pot roast. There are so many options. We're sharing our favorite family dinner recipes with you in chapter 17. Before you know it, you'll add your own favorites to the list!

Is Baby Getting Enough?

At this stage, babies should be sitting down with the family, or caregivers, two to three meals per day. Whether baby eats is up to them. The Division of Responsibility for this age suggests the parent or caregiver is responsible for *what* food will be offered while baby decides on *how much* to eat.[3] While you're enjoying your own meal, you're demonstrating how to chew and savor each bite of new food. Now that you've expanded baby's variety, you may notice that he's excited to see new foods or maybe even unsure at the sight of new mixed meal. But that's okay. Continue to consistently offer the new foods.

Since baby is in charge of how much to eat without feeding help or coaching him to eat more, we as parents can begin to worry if he's getting enough. If baby is still taking milk feedings and starting to actually eat some of his offered foods during meal or snack times, it's very likely that baby's growth, measured by length and weight at the pediatrician's office, is right on track for *his* individual body. Babies follow their own growth curves; some stay at the same percentile curve throughout infancy while others may have bumps higher or lower visit to visit. If your child has a large bump up or down on the curve, this can be concerning, but is often normal within the first six months (and even up to age two). Sometimes it can be a fluke, a bout of sickness, or even a measurement error. Regardless, it's a good idea to follow up and repeat the measures so you and your pediatrician can determine the next steps. Purposeful weight loss is never a goal.

Should You Worry about the Weight?

Growth around a stable percentile is reassuring, but it is not uncommon for babies' weight to shift up or down on the growth chart within the first six months and even up to two years of age.[4,5] Family doctor and childhood feeding specialist Dr. Katja Rowell says, "While weight loss and sudden changes are always worrisome, if baby is doing well overall, weight percentiles moving up or down isn't always concerning, but warrants a thorough history and exam." This is an important tidbit for us as parents because as soon as a doctor puts a label like *underweight*, *overweight*, or *obese* on our kids, we're going to worry and be tempted to take our feeding strategy in a different direction–our doctors might even ask us to. This can lead to food pushing if our little one is labeled underweight or restricting if labeled overweight, which is likely to backfire (more on this in chapter 8).

>>

Where your child is weight-wise may be exactly where they need to be no matter the label. *Underweight* and *obese* labels sound scary, but if baby is bigger or smaller than average and growing in a steady way, that is likely to be healthy.[6] We've seen many clients where a misguided worry about weight led to feeding problems and can make weight problems worse. We are *Born to Eat*, and with that comes times of learning, growth, and weight fluctuations. Many children also gain weight before height, so checking growth over time is essential. Remember that responsive feeding and the *Born to Eat* way is linked with more healthy weight patterns. If there's something amiss in terms of weight, you and your doctor can address it; otherwise, worrying about weight usually makes it harder to feed the *Born to Eat* way. Helping your baby get plenty of sleep and love, limiting screen time, and finding ways to help them move their bodies in active play will help him grow in a healthy way.

Development Through Food Exploration

These are exciting times. Hopefully, you and baby are getting the swing of self-feeding and feeling more confident about the baby-led weaning approach. As parents, we're learning our role in the feeding process while baby is learning his role. Most likely, he's also learning and developing loads of skills right before your eyes.

The pincer grasp, which may start around six or seven months, is usually more efficient around nine to twelve months. During this stage, you can watch how baby is progressing from a clumsy grasp to a more fine movement. As finger dexterity improves, baby will be able to feed himself more efficiently. This allows baby to pick up foods with his thumb and forefinger just like CC was starting to do with her beans. Baby's fine motor skills will quickly become stronger and he may also want to use a utensil, though more likely he will hold utensil with one hand and feed with the other. Around this same time, baby also develops a love for throwing. Be prepared for flying objects! Cause and effect are fun at this age, so when your baby tests how quickly that sweet potato wedge can drop to the floor, don't fret—it's normal, it's expected, and it's truly is a part of the learning process. Just have another slice on the ready because he'll quickly realize he can't get that one back to eat.

American Sign Language and Feeding

If you're interested in using American Sign Language with your baby, which we both did, this is an excellent time to introduce these helpful food-related signs. We found these signs very helpful in understanding baby's cues and supporting responsive eating before baby talks.

<u>All finished or all done:</u> holding both hands up and waving them. When your baby is starting to throw more things off the table then put to their mouth, then it's a great time to ask if they're all finished. Be sure to give them some time to process the question before taking their food away.

<u>More:</u> bring fingers to your thumbs on both hands then tap thumbs while keeping your hands in this position.

<u>Milk:</u> squeeze your hands like you are milking an udder on a cow.

<u>Water:</u> make a W with your fingers and bring it to your lips. This isn't exclusive to water you drink, so you can talk about water as it relates to a pool, rain, a puddle, or in the bath.

<u>Food or eat:</u> pinch fingers to thumb and bring up to your mouth. "It's time to eat," is a great way to indicate mealtime and using this sign.

>>

The more consistently you use these signs, the quicker your baby will grasp them and use the signs to ease communication barriers. Your baby may not master the sign until they have excellent finger dexterity, so look for any evidence that they are trying to use the sign and praise them with utter excitement to encourage them to continue trying and using sign language. For example, Miss A still signed the word *water* by bringing only one finger up to her mouth at sixteen months old, but it was also her first sign at seven months old. She would also use the sign for water any time she wanted to sip what mom and dad were drinking.

Chapter 6 References

1. Jisheng Gao, Hongwei Wu, Jinfeng Liu, "Importance of gut microbiota in health and diseases of new born infants (Review)," *Experimental and Therapeutic Medicine* 12(1): (July 2016): 28–32, published online April 11, 2016, doi: 10.3892/etm.2016.3253 PMCID: PMC4906629.

2. Martin Frederik Laursen, Louise B. B. Andersen, Kim F. Michaelsen, Christian Mølgaard, Ellen Trolle, Martin Iain Bahl, Tine Rask Licht, "Host-Microbe Biology Infant Gut Microbiota Development Is Driven by Transition to Family Foods Independent of Maternal Obesity," *mSphere* 1(1) (January–February 2016): e00069-15. Published online 2016 Feb 10. doi: 10.1128/mSphere.00069-15 PMCID: PMC4863607http://www.ncbi.nlm.nih.gov/pmc/articles/PMC4863607/.

3. "Ellyn Satter's Division of Responsibility in Feeding," Ellyn Satter Institute, accessed September 20, 2016, http://ellynsatterinstitute.org/dor/divisionofresponsibilityin-feeding.php.

4. Arthur Jaffe, "Failure to Thrive: Current Clinical Concepts," *Pediatrics in Review*, 32(3), (March 2011): 100–107. DOI: 10.1542/pir.32-3-100.

5. Zuguo Mei, Laurence Grummer-Strawn, Diane Thompson, William Dietz, "Shifts in Percentiles of Growth During Early Childhood: Analysis of Longitudinal Data From the California Child Health and Development Study," *Pediatrics*, 113 (6), (June 2004): e617–e627, accessed article October 12, 2016.

6. James Ledler, Lewis Rose, "Assessment of Abnormal Growth Curves," *American Family Physician*, 58(1), (July 1998): 153–158, accessed article October 12, 2016. http://ellynsatterinstitute.org/dor/divisionofresponsibilityinfeeding.php http://ellynsatterinstitute.org/dor/divisionofresponsibilityinfeeding.php

CHAPTER 7

THIS STUFF IS TASTY
(9 TO 12 MONTHS—THE NOVICE)

> "Adopt the pace of nature: her secret is patience."
> —Ralph Waldo Emerson

Leslie took CC to the office a couple times a week. CC loved looking around at all the nutritionist stuff while Leslie did administrative tasks or met with other dietitians in the office. CC was about ten months old and eating like a champ. Leslie carried snacks like peeled clementines with her because CC loved them. One day, while Leslie was having a discussion with a coworker, she could tell CC was hungry so she gave her a piece of the clementine. A few seconds later, Leslie noticed that she was too quiet and looked over to see CC's scared, red face, and watering eyes. Leslie quickly grabbed CC out of her car seat and a set her upright. CC was able to control the clementine and swallow it with no problem once she was sitting upright. They'd both gotten a bit too comfortable since she had been self-feeding so well, and Leslie didn't think a thing about giving CC a snack while reclined in her car seat. This was a very scary (and embarrassing) lesson in feeding safety, and Leslie never did that again! It could happen to any one of us, even a nutrition pro.

At this stage, it's tempting to be more relaxed with food just because you've seen them gain skills, make great strides, and begin to eat like a toddler. But the truth is they're still babies and they get tired, get overly excited, or can be too relaxed. It's always important to stay tuned in while your little one eats. We feel it's important to remind caregivers and ourselves that attention toward monitoring little ones is still a priority while they continue on their eating journeys.

Milestones

From crawling to walking to teething, your little one is likely reaching huge milestones in the final three months of her first year. She's really starting to master her pincer grasp and is able to pick up the tiny blueberry or a pitted cherry and plop it in her mouth. She's probably getting confident in her own skills at this point and may be excited to use utensils, too. This is all part of the natural progression of raising babies who are *Born to Eat*. What you offer also helps her master skills to become a much neater eater, but she's not quite there yet.

In addition to finger dexterity, you will notice your little one might be a bit more active at this age, as she's learning to stand or possibly walk or still mastering her crawl. Because of this need to move, you may find keeping her in her high chair to be a bit more challenging. It's tempting to put their food on the ground and let them graze, but as convenient as it may seem, babies are more apt to choke unless seated properly while eating. If your little one wants to move, let her down and then ask again if she's ready to eat in five or ten minutes (this is the perfect time to sign *food* or *more*). If not, you can put the food away and try again later. A baby's attention span is short, but she'll likely let you know when she's hungry again, or her fussing will be your first clue.

To help at mealtimes, try engaging your little one around food by introducing food to her or try playing a game of peek-a-boo with foods on her plate to get her interested in sitting at the table. This helps with creating habits, and by having your little one eat with you at meals, she's growing more accustomed to this behavior and will be more apt to sit longer and longer at a meal with each passing month.

Trust your intuition and assessment of your little one's progression. Find a pediatrician you trust and they'll have no problem with you being a proactive parent versus a reactive one. Keep track of areas of concern to share with your pediatrician and have things written out prior to your appointment. This can keep you both on track so you don't feel rushed or pass over a concern.

Chomp Chomp

Teething is likely in full swing by now. Even if teeth haven't popped yet, your little one is probably gumming everything in sight and drooling like a river. She may want to put everything in her mouth to help find relief for her aching gums or just enjoy the sensation of something new. Food items and non-food items are a challenge to decipher for a teething baby or toddler on the move. Wendy Jo's pediatrician, Dr. Dave, shared a great tip with her.

Dr. Dave says it's best to go around the house with an empty toilet paper roll and remove anything off the floor that could possibly fit through the hole, as anything smaller than that hole can fit nicely down your little one's throat. Thanks, Dr. Dave!

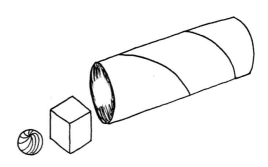

Babies get teeth at varying times; some may have six by now and some may not even have one. If you stick your finger in their mouth, they'll be sure to show you how well they can gum. *OUCH!* Great teething foods include frozen and slightly thawed bananas, cold cucumber sticks, or a cold slice of steak. Just like at every other stage, each baby is different. Wendy Jo's little one had a taste for sand, leaves, rocks, and basically anything she get her hands on while CC wasn't much of a chewer of things other than food.

Now that we've covered some milestones, let's see whether a baby is ready to move ahead with her eating. If all of a sudden you notice your little one is not wanting to eat as much or crying out when eating, don't assume they're becoming picky eaters. It's not uncommon for a baby to turn down food while teething, as it may hurt their gums until the tooth breaks through the gum line. If they're nursing, or have a greater desire for formula instead of food, chalk it up to teething. During this time, keep offering foods, more breast milk or formula feedings, and in time, they'll return to their normal eating patterns.

> Wendy Jo's daughter had three days where she would only choose to eat softer foods offered on her plate, like berries and yogurt, then *pop!* There was her first tooth.

With the addition of new teeth, your little one may be ready for some new textures. Up to this point, vegetables and fruit were very soft. It may be time to try a crunchier green bean, a wedge of cantaloupe, or steamed broccoli. If she's ready, she will take little nibbles, chew up each piece, and continue on with her meal. If she's not ready for this texture, she may gag or spit out the food and leave it on her plate. Keep offering a new texture every couple days so she can continue to work on the skill and let you know when she's ready to advance. All skills take practice, and no one is an expert at first bite. Your little one is entering into the novice stage of eating.

Is Baby Ready?

Baby Dayne was nine months old. He'd been fidgety and fussy sitting through mealtimes and crying when he took a bite of food. He had a couple new teeth erupting.

- ❏ Ready
- ✔ Not Ready, new teeth can make it a challenge to try out new foods. Give Baby Dayne a couple more weeks or until the pain of new teeth fade.

Baby Simone was ten months old and blueberries were her new favorite food. She loved picking up one blueberry half at a time and could easily eat ½ cup or more at breakfast.

- ✔ Ready, looks like Baby Simone has the pincer grasp now.
- ❏ Not Ready

Baby Maya was nine months old. She was served a steamed green bean just like her parents like them, *al dente*. At first bite, she chewed, made a gagging noise, and spit out the green bean. She went for her raspberry instead and left the green bean on her plate.

- ❏ Ready
- ✔ Not Ready, advancing Baby Maya to an al dente texture may be a bit early. Steam her green beans a bit longer and try again in a couple weeks. Bravo to Baby Maya for recognizing this and spitting out her green bean.

Now that you have a better idea where your novice eater is in regards to progression of eating, let's review our safety checklist for this skill level. You will note that some things have changed as your little grows and has more skills.

Novice Safety Checklist

1. Secure baby upright in a high chair or feeding seat. Baby should never be reclined, eating in a car seat (thank you, Leslie, for that reminder), or eating in someone's lap. This allows the parent or caregiver to evaluate how baby is doing at all times.
2. **Never** leave baby alone when eating. It's more tempting to turn your back while she's eating at this age or feed her on the floor, but risks are still present and it's best to tune in to each bite.
3. Let baby put food in her mouth. She needs to be in control of how fast the food enters her mouth or how much she eats at all times. As tempting as it is, especially if baby slows eating a bit with teething, you don't have to help. As baby progresses with eating a variety of foods, she may still need some coaching to chew or spit out foods.
4. If the food has been cooked, continue to test the temperature of the food to ensure it has cooled enough for baby to test. Even something perceived as warm by the caregiver may be felt as hot by a baby. She may be able to handle warmer items and be taught to blow on her food to cool down a hot bite.
5. She may now be ready for vegetables that are a bit more al dente over very soft vegetables. Let her test the new texture and advance as you see fit.
6. Foods can now be offered in smaller pieces, about the size of a pinky nail or in wedges, depending on the food.
7. Don't offer foods that easily break off into small pieces or crumbs that could potentially block the airway of baby, as they can pose a choking risk. Foods we recommend still avoiding at *this stage* due to increased risk of choking include raw apples, whole grapes, whole cherry tomatoes, other raw fruits or vegetables with tough skins, nuts, thick nut-butters, popcorn, marshmallows, hard candy, hot dogs, very crusty bread, or any food in a round or coin-like shape.

What Goes In Must Come Out

We're dietitians and have no problem talking about your little one's food exit strategy. Let's talk poo—appropriate potty talk, of course. With the advances in your little one's eating, you'll notice changes in her diaper. As gross as it can be, a diaper has a story to tell. A baby who still is taking in more formula or breast milk has a more yellow hue to the poop; whereas a baby who is eating more has very identifiable food in the

poo (*poo* sounds a lot better than *fecal matter* or *stools*). The color will become darker brown and will start to take on a more solid form. You may not have the same perception and wish to discard that stinky diaper as quick as can be—we get it—but the diaper speaks volumes about food intake. Randomly pick a day and check out the contents. This will help you know whether your little one is eating more food over just playing with the plate or tossing it overboard to feed her favorite pooch. It will also give you an indication of how well she's chewing up the food before swallowing. Does a blueberry half make its way out? Perhaps cut them in half, if so. Or, are you finding beans make their way out just as they went in? Again, a good time to cut the bean in half.

As gross as it is, poo can provide some value in letting the parent know just how well a little one is eating. Again, as icky as this may sound, your pediatrician may ask you questions about this and you'll know exactly why.

Now that you know the basic ins and outs of poo, it's time to discuss the nutrients your little one needs at this time to continue to thrive. Remember, the *Born to Eat* team doesn't advocate eating nutrients. We, as humans, eat whole foods versus single nutrients. Ramp up the offerings of whole foods to ensure the baby is getting adequate nutrition.

Grow Baby, Grow

As you have probably noticed, your baby has been rapidly changing sizes in baby clothes and their little head keeps growing. With all that growing, two additional key nutrients to focus on over the next couple months are zinc and selenium. We've touched on zinc before, but we're digging a little deeper now.

These two nutrients are antioxidant powerhouses, meaning they inhibit oxidation at the cellular level. Antioxidants are important in fighting cell damage by free radicals. Antioxidants, such as zinc and selenium, are important dietary additions for your growing infant. As your baby continues to grow, so will their appetite, making it easier to get in a greater variety of nutrients. Don't fret if your baby isn't able to eat as much; they continue to get their bulk of nutrients from breast milk or formula.

Zinc

Wendy Jo's college professor loved to say, "I Zinc Therefore I am." A little play on words, but definitely gives way to showing the importance of this antioxidant. Zinc plays an important role in metabolism and digestion and is often linked to skin issues, such as eczema. The good news is, if you've stuck to our suggestions of first foods, your baby is getting in ample, because beef is a star player in delivering zinc—just 1-ounce delivers exactly what your baby needs. Other solid zinc providers include beans, almond butter (she's not quite ready for whole or chopped nuts), yogurt, ricotta cheese, and peas. Red meat takes center stage for zinc, but the rest are great sources, too.

If you're concerned about taking in too much zinc, don't be. When you stick with foods in their whole food form, it's hard to chew too much zinc-rich food. People, regardless of age, are more at risk of overdoing nutrients when they add in many fortified foods or supplements. We recommend sticking with whole-food sources unless your doctor suggests otherwise.

Selenium

Selenium is a key antioxidant involved with vitamin C, thyroid health, and the body's response to stress. When a body comes under stress, the need for selenium increases because selenium is part of the glutathione peroxidases enzyme mechanism (what?!).

In short, it's a big deal when our body is dealing with severe stress. Breast milk has selenium, so if you have continued breastfeeding, your little one is still taking in selenium. Selenium wasn't always a mandatory ingredient in infant formula. According to the Food and Drug Administration's official website, selenium was added to the mandated list of nutrients in infant formulas in June 2015. Selenium is a big deal, but a small amount goes a long way.

Just like an adult, the recommendation for including seafood in an infant and child's diet is about two to three times per week. If you keep this in mind, your baby is most likely getting in ample selenium. Seafood is one of the top sources of selenium and can be found in tuna, shrimp, and salmon. If you're not able to eat seafood or enjoy it as frequently as suggested, selenium can also be found in mushrooms, asparagus, eggs, turkey, chicken, and sunflower seeds.

How Much Is Enough? Or Too Much?

One of the most frequent questions the *Born to Eat* team gets is in regard to quantity of food. How much is enough food for a baby? The truth is the range in amounts will vary, and a nine-month-old may or may not eat as much as a twelve month old, and Johnny next door may eat less than Sue down the street but more than Robbie from daycare. The goal is that by the time baby hits their first birthday, they can sustain themselves with foods, transition to whole cow's milk from a cup, and no longer need breast milk or formula. We will cover more on that in the next chapter. But remember, breastfeeding duration is like what you chew—it's up to you (and your little one). Rest assured, your little one is working on eating more, developing precise self-feeding skills, and learning from you every time you sit down to a enjoy a meal together.

Dishing it Up

By now, you're seeing that your baby truly can enjoy eating exactly what you eat without making special meals or only serving up kid-friendly foods. At this stage, baby can likely transition from isolated foods like spaghetti with meatballs on the side to normally plated mixed meals like

Spaghetti and Meatballs
Finger of Bread
4 Green Beans

spaghetti with meatballs on top. Remember, it's best to put less on a plate so your little one doesn't get overwhelmed. But don't forget to offer seconds and even thirds if your little one indicates they want more (reaching for more, signing more, opening mouth, sucking on fist). We don't want to overwhelm baby, and we sure don't want to restrict them either (this can lead to food preoccupation later on). If baby is leading the way, baby will likely eat to meet her needs. Sometimes she'll eat a lot and other times a little. Here is a sample three-day menu for your nine- to twelve-month-old. Note the range in amounts that you can start with and offer more as needed.

Meal	Sample Day 1	Sample Day 2	Sample Day 3
Breakfast	❑ ½–1 boiled egg ❑ 2 Tablespoons–¼ cup plain, whole fat, Greek yogurt ❑ 2 Tablespoons–¼ cup blueberries	❑ 1 slice (cut into thin strips) thinly smeared almond butter toast ❑ 1 mini-muffin frittata (pg 182) ❑ 5–10 raspberries	❑ 2 Tablespoons–¼ cup ground beef sausage (pg 192) ❑ 2 Tablespoons sweet potato hash brown ❑ 2–4 strawberries
Snack	❑ 2 Tablespoons hummus ❑ 2 pretzels	❑ ¼ cup whole grain O cereal ❑ 2 Tablespoons–¼ cup plain, whole fat, Greek yogurt	❑ 2 Tablespoons applesauce ❑ ¼ cup grated cheese
Lunch	❑ 2 Tablespoons–¼ cup tuna fish salad (pg 198) ❑ ⅛–¼ avocado slices or mashed and spread on bread or crackers ❑ 2 whole grain crackers or ½ slice whole-grain bread ❑ 2 Tablespoons canned (in juice or water) mandarin oranges	❑ ¼ cup lentil soup ❑ ¼ grilled cheese sandwich (cut into ½-inch bites) ❑ ¼–½ kiwi fruit	❑ 2 Tablespoons–¼ cup cottage or ricotta cheese ❑ 2–4 zucchini finger fritters ❑ 2–3 cherry tomato halves with olive oil and lemon juice ❑ 4–6 blackberries

Meal	Sample Day 1	Sample Day 2	Sample Day 3
Snack	❑ 2 Tablespoons cottage or ricotta cheese ❑ ¼ very ripe pear or 1 very small pear that baby can hold to eat	❑ ¼–½ boiled egg or egg salad ❑ 1–2 whole grain crackers	❑ 1 (2-inch) cucumber spear ❑ 2–4 quartered olives, without seed ❑ 2–4 Tablespoons whole fat, plain Greek yogurt
Dinner	❑ ¼–½ cup spaghetti with meat sauce	❑ ½–1 whole grilled salmon patties ❑ 2–4 steamed green beans ❑ ¼ cup oven roasted potato wedges	❑ ¼–½ cup chicken pot pie (pg 219) ❑ 1 square dark chocolate

In real life, it looks a little different for every family. CC ate a good serving of fruit and eggs most mornings shortly after waking while Miss A had breakfast broken up into two snack-like meals. Times are not carved in stone nor are the number of meals offered. What is certain is that your little one has a smaller stomach and does need to eat more frequently than adults. From nine to twelve months of age, your little one will be moving toward eating roughly three meals and two to three snacks per day. Don't feel as though you ever have to follow this like it's a diet or scripted meal plan. It's not! The idea of this meal plan menu example is to show variety and that your baby can eat what you eat. It's only ever too much if they're being pressured to eat more than they want at that eating opportunity.

You Choose What, They Choose How Much

Just like the beginner eater, Ellyn Satter's Division of Responsibility holds true for this age, as well. The Division of Responsibility suggests the parent or caregiver is responsible for *what* food will be offered while baby decides on *how much* to eat. Our perception of what is enough may not match what baby really wants or needs. If you feel they're not eating enough, offer meals more frequently throughout the day, offer high-fat, nutrient-dense foods, and skip beverages until after mealtimes (liquids can be too filling and cause lower intake of solid foods at meals). At this point, you can avoid nursing or giving infant formula to your baby until after they've finished their meal.

Time Flies

Congrats! You're off to a great start, and your baby has an excellent foundation for eating. Next up is baby's first birthday, and with that comes a toddler with an independent mind and palate. The *Born to Eat* team has you covered, and chapters 8 and 9 tackle the more selective palate and creative ways to keep your toddler on the self-feeding path.

CHAPTER 8

I'M ON THE MOVE
(12 TO 24 MONTHS–THE
PRE-ADVANCED EATER)

> "Silence is golden–unless you have a toddler. In that case,
> silence is very, very suspicious."
>
> —Anonymous

The cake smash. It's the one-year-old's rite of passage into the food world. Hopefully by the time your little one smears icing across his hair and anyone nearby, he has experienced much of what the family table has to offer. And in every possible texture. This can be such a fun time for food adventuring and dining as a family. Not only is he eating a variety of foods and textures, but he's likely hungry for more since he can walk and explore on his own. He may also decide he'd rather explore than eat. Your baby has graduated to a toddler and his rate of growth development has slowed down, so if you do notice a drop in intake, don't let it get you overly concerned; on the other hand, if his newly found ability to walk has turned into a run, then his eating may be off and running, too.

It's possible you're feeling like you have this feeding thing down! We sure did. Year One can lead to many food adventures for you and the little one, like ordering from a real menu. Before he orders that chicken Parmesan, let's take a moment to see how this new toddler is progressing with feeding skills, texture tolerance, and food intake. Use this checklist to determine if your toddler is ready to move from a novice eater to the pre-advanced eater. By now, your little one is likely:

- Eating 3 meals and 2 to 3 snacks per day
- Grasping items with a fine pincer grasp
- Handling almost all textures
- Biting and chewing most foods
- Holding and using a spoon more effectively
- Able to eat most of his meal but may start leaving more on plate
- Moving away from a sippy or straw cups to an open cup with all meals
- Using more control getting food into his mouth and spilling less
- Asking for more food as needed

Remember, each toddler is developing at his own pace. These are general markers of progressing in feeding and eating skills. Now that he's more mobile and having tons of fun around the house, we have to keep in mind new or changing areas of concern. Let's review safety now that your little one has graduated to a toddler or pre-advanced eater.

The Pre-Advanced Eater Safety Checklist

1. Toddler eats at the table in high chair, not walking around or while playing.
2. Turn off distractions, such as television or a toy, so he can focus on his food. Distractions can lead to accidents while eating, in addition to creating a habit of mindless eating.
3. **Never** leave him unattended while eating. Although his feeding skills have improved dramatically, it's a good idea to stay close while eating. Depending on how many teeth he has and his chewing competency, choking can still be a risk.
4. Continue to test the temperature of cooked and mixed meals to make sure they're not too hot for him to handle. Just like testing with texture, you can teach him to test by taking a bite or placing it to his lip.
5. Foods can be offered in smaller pieces now that your little one is chewing more efficiently. For example, instead of fingers of steak, you can cut into smaller bites. Although children don't get their grinding molars until about two to three years old, they can gum, gnaw, and chew meats quite well, especially with preparations that keep it moist and tender.
6. Foods that were once avoided whole can be included depending on your little one's chewing development. If needed, you can still cut round foods like grapes

(in halves from stem end to point, not around the middle), cherry tomatoes, hot dogs, etc. in half.

7. There still may be foods that are hard for your toddler to manipulate with his gums, teeth, or chewing skills. Modify the texture as needed—like pulling the strings from an orange section or chopping nuts.

Is Little One Ready to Move On?

Let's look and see if your little one is ready to move into pre-advanced eating.

Little Debbie used to struggled with her spoon while eating her oatmeal at breakfast and enjoyed using her hands instead. Occasionally she would try the spoon throughout the meal.

❑ Ready
✔ Not Ready, Little Debbie needs more time working with her spoon skills.

Little Johnny is doing great using his open cup and spoon during most meals. He's now able to eat thin liquids, like soup with his spoon with minimum spillage.

✔ Ready. Little Johnny seems to be eating well with his spoon.
❑ Not Ready

Little Maxie is using her baby signs to ask for more food at mealtimes. She seems to be honoring her own hunger cues in a growing body.

✔ Ready. Little Maxie is eating well and getting used to honoring her body's cues.
❑ Not Ready

Don't Freak Out

For the last year, you've likely watched your baby become a happy and interested eater. It isn't uncommon for this interest and appetite to decrease, though. This is normal since the growth velocity has slowed dramatically from those early months of life. When we've counseled parents of one- to two-year-olds, we often hear that they wished they had known that was normal. We love our kids and want them to be nourished. It's very tempting to stray from the Division of Responsibility when we feel desperate for them to eat or to get enough. We've been tempted to say "just one more bite" or "just finish your carrots," as well, but we have to trust that the same intuition that helped them feed themselves to this point will also help them stay nourished enough to sustain their growth and development by self-regulation. They are *Born to Eat*, and their bodies will respond accordingly.

Research suggests that a controlling parenting style, whether it's pushing a child to eat more or restricting their intake, leads to poor self-regulation.[1] It seems that controlling parental styles have the exact opposite outcome of what the parent is trying to control. If the diet is being restricted, it's very likely the child will eat more when given the chance and is linked to increased weight gain. However, if the child is pressured to eat, those behaviors can result in difficulty eating, less enjoyment of food, and becoming underweight. The bottom line is, no matter how strong the urge is to control our little one's intake can be, make every attempt to avoid it. After all, we're *Born to Eat,* and the Division of Responsibility can help keep us, parents and little ones alike, on track.

Let's take a moment to review our role as a parent following the Division of Responsibility supporting a self-regulating eater. Parents remain in charge of *when* food is offered, *what* food is offered, and *where* it will be eaten or served. An additional role on our part is to *trust*. Trust that our *Born to Eat* child can do just that and follow their role. We're trusting that our little one will follow his role to decide *whether or if* he'll eat and *how much*. We've watched these beautiful skills develop in the families we've counseled along with our own kids. It's totally doable.

Breaking down the roles at a meal may look a bit like this scenario. Mom makes dinner at six o'clock (when) and puts roasted sweet potatoes, asparagus, strawberries, and barbeque chicken (what) on David's plate. Dad sets the table in the kitchen (where). David gets seated in his high chair and begins to eat his sweet potatoes, strawberries, and chicken (whether). He's unsure about the asparagus but explores. He left most of the asparagus and half of his sweet potatoes on his plate (how much) and pushed it away to signal that he was

finished. Mom and Dad have seen him eat everything on his dinner plate with the exact same menu. Although they're concerned about him getting enough, they trust he's self-regulating for his needs at that moment and don't encourage him to eat more. David and his parents are respecting their roles and trusting each other in their responsibilities.

Nutrition versus Nutrients

Now that your little one is a year old, it's recommended to add whole cow's milk as a beverage in place of infant formula. Some may still be breastfeeding on demand or putting breast milk in a cup and that's cool, too. Do what works best for you and your little one. Just remember that beverages like milk can fill your little one's tummy quickly and decrease the amount of food eaten at a meal. Milk can be offered with a small snack or after the meal so more solid foods may be eaten.

To Drink or Not to Drink

Another frequent question that comes up around this time is about beverages. Fruit juices are a hot-button topic. If you choose to use juice at this age, be sure that the juice you choose is 100 percent fruit juice. Dilute this juice as much as you possibly can, perhaps 1 ounce of juice in an 8-ounce glass filled with 7 ounces water. We do believe some juices have a benefit and a possible place in a child's life. After all, many of us enjoy the occasional diversion from water. Of 100 percent juice options, our top picks serve a purpose and can complement an occasional meal or a snack. We've added small amounts of these juices to yogurt, water, cooked foods, oats, and popsicles to add flavor changes and functional benefits. The nutrients delivered in 1 to 2 ounces of these juices per day aren't easily attainable through whole foods:

- ❑ Concord Grape Juice—The benefits an adult can get from drinking wine can be found in the dark juices of Concord grapes. From research on brain function to heart health, Concord grapes have been earning a lot of positive press for their nutritional attributes.[2,3]
- ❑ Tart Cherry Juice—It may be too tart for your palate, but may be just right for your little one. Tart cherry juice may help with sleep, so perhaps reserve the 1- to 2-ounce serving for after dinner.[4]

>>

❑   Cranberry Juice–Another tart juice with promising research. Cranberry juice may help prevent recurrent urinary tract infections in adults and children alike.[5]

❑   Orange Juice–Ditch the orange-flavored beverages and opt for the real deal. Orange juice offers a great source of vitamin C, and if your little one hasn't fallen in love with meats and you're using beans or vegetables as key protein sources, this will complement your meal to help with the absorption of iron from other food sources.

With each offering of something to drink, this is a great time to introduce an open cup and a hard straw (hard plastic or stainless steel). Here's another trick from Dr. Dave: place a straw in a cup of water and cover the straw opening with a finger. While holding your finger in place, give it to your infant and allow them to suck the beverage from the straw before releasing your finger. This can aid in teaching your little one how to suck up liquids from a straw. Some babies take to this quickly, and others may require more frequent introductions. For those who prefer straws, you'll find excellent metal and multi-use straws on the market that are dishwasher safe.

We've mentioned before that we eat food, not nutrients. While our foods provide great nutrients, we don't sit down to a plate of vitamin C and omega-3 fatty acids. We're sitting down to grilled salmon and roasted red peppers. Now that your little one is a year old, his meals are likely looking a lot like yours except on a smaller scale. When we're thinking of nutrients and nutrition overall, we can focus on the same thing we'd want you to focus on for the whole family: balance. If you were sitting across from us in our respective counseling offices, we'd tell you to fill your plate with colorful fruits and vegetables, muscle-supporting proteins, satisfying fats, and energy-giving carbohydrates. And the way we teach it is visual, just like creating that first plate for baby. We use the Plate Method. A variety of organizations and associations use a similar way of teaching a balanced plate, but this is how we use the Plate Method.

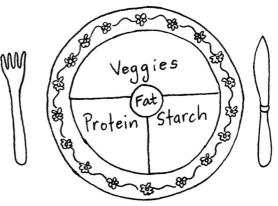

First, visualize your plate. We're using a typical round plate. Cut the plate in half and that's where you'll put your vegetables and fruits. Then cut the other half in half again. Now we've got about a quarter of your plate for your muscle-supporting protein and a quarter for your energy-giving carbohydrates. We'll pop our satisfying fats right on top. We're not leaving out dairy; we just happen to throw it in with protein. It makes it easier (and tasty).

Balance is important, but even the best eaters don't have perfect plates every day. And that's okay (and normal)! We've both experienced a meal where our little ones only eat the sweet potatoes or the brownie. As parents (and nutrition experts) we, of course, want our kids to have a balanced diet; however, the *how* a child eats, developing feeding and eating behaviors early on, may be even more important than the *what* they eat in the beginning. In our nutrition counseling offices, we've seen the damage that the lack of body trust can cause over time. These early years can be so important in feeding and eating behavior development. Once we trust and support the self-regulating *how* of eating, the *what*, or balance, will likely come in time.

> What we eat is important, but having a hyper focus on eating certain foods, or not eating certain foods, can backfire. When food is a big deal, it may always be a big deal.

It's common during this time for your little one to have more preferences. He may only eat the eggs on his breakfast plate and not the toast. This is also okay. As parents, we continue to offer the foods even though we know that he may not eat it from one day to the next. Many parents worry at this stage that their children may be becoming picky eaters. There's typical picky eating, which is normal like described above, and then there's extreme picky eating. Sometimes a typical picky eating sixteen-month-old will start eating fewer and fewer foods or textures.

There are a variety of reasons for this, and as parents, we don't want to make a normal issue a problematic one. For example, say CC stopped eating broccoli (she did) for a while and we stopped offering it to her saying she's picky (we didn't). Then the same thing happens with tomatoes, and we say "Oh, she's picky and won't eat those foods." It's possible we took a typical one-year-old eater and helped create a very picky one. Remember, when food's a big deal, it's a big deal.

Is It Typical Picky Eating or Extreme?

About half of all young children are considered "picky" at some point. Most picky eating behaviors are part of normal eating stages. All parents need more information and support to identify typical picky eating, how not to make matters worse, how to support a healthy relationship to food, when to seek professional help, and how to find the right help. We define *extreme picky eating* (EPE) as not eating enough quantity or variety to support healthy emotional, physical, or social development; or eating patterns that are a significant source of conflict or worry. Extreme picky eating is an umbrella term that covers labels including: *selective eating, food aversion, feeding disorder, ARFID* (avoidant restrictive food intake disorder), *problem feeder*, and *infantile anorexia* (older term).

Anything that makes getting food to the mouth, chewing, swallowing, and digesting difficult, painful, or uncomfortable increases the odds a child will struggle with more extreme picky eating. How a child is fed also plays a critical role. Here are some signs that parents may be dealing with more extreme picky eating, often linked with medical challenges, oral-motor or sensory difficulties, anxiety, autism spectrum, temperament, and feeding history. These are complex problems with many factors that must be considered and addressed.

- ❑ Not able to gum or chew with molars by 15 to 18 months
- ❑ Falling off growth curve, losing weight
- ❑ Struggled with breast or bottle feeding and/or transition to solids (versus the child who does well until 15 to 18 months when typical picky eating phase usually starts)
- ❑ Choking, vomiting regularly, aspirating
- ❑ Pain or distress with eating or digesting
- ❑ Pocketing or "cheeking" food (functional or behavioral)
- ❑ Avoids entire food groups
- ❑ Stuck at a transition, e.g., can't get beyond spoon or purées
- ❑ Small number of "safe" or accepted foods, may be particular packaging or brand
- ❑ Child is anxious or upset out of proportion, beyond typical toddler tantrum
- ❑ Showed little interest in food/eating all along
- ❑ Never mouthed foods or objects (sensorimotor clues)
- ❑ Can't go to sleepovers or parties due to limited accepted food and/or anxiety

❏ Teased by peers, or extreme attention from adults (family, teachers) around child's eating

❏ History of forced or pressured feeding and reluctance to eat

From Dr. Katja Rowell, feeding expert and author, with coauthor Jenny McGlothlin SLP. *Helping Your Child with Extreme Picky Eating: A Step-by-Step Guide for Overcoming Selective Eating, Food Aversion, and Feeding Disorders.*

CHAPTER 8 REFERENCES

1. Brown, A. and Lee, M. D. (2015), Early influences on child satiety-responsiveness: the role of weaning style. *Pediatric Obesity*, 10: 57–66. doi:10.1111/j.2047-6310.2013.00207.x

2. Daniel J. Lamport, Claire L. Lawton, Natasha Merat, Hamish Jamson, Kyriaki Myrissa, Denise Hofman, Helen K. Chadwick, Frits Quadt, JoLynne D. Wightman, Louise Dye, "Concord grape juice, cognitive function, and driving performance: a 12-wk, placebo-controlled, randomized crossover trial in mothers of preteen children," *American Journal of Clinical Nutrition* 103(3) (March 2016): 775–83, date of Epublication February 10, 2016, doi: 10.3945/ajcn.115.114553.

3. Lisa M. Vislocky and Maria Louise Fernandez, "Grapes and Grape Products: Their Role in Health." *Nutrition Today* 48 (1) (2013): 47–51, DOI: 10.1111/j.1753-4887.2010.00335.x

4. G Howatson, PG Bell, J Tallent, B Middleton, MP McHugh, J Ellis, "Effect of tart cherry juice (Prunus cerasus) on melatonin levels and enhanced sleep quality," *European Journal of Nutrition* 51 (8) (December 2012): 909–16, ePublication October 30, 2011, doi: 10.1007/s00394-011-0263-7.

5. Ran D. Goldman, "Cranberry juice for urinary tract infection in children," *Canadian Family Physician* 58(4) (April 2012): 398–401, accessed article October 5, 2016, http://www.cfp.ca/content/58/4/398.full.

CHAPTER 9

I DON'T LIKE THAT . . . TODAY
(24 TO 36 MONTHS–THE ADVANCED EATER)

> "Affirming words from moms and dads are like light switches. Speak a word of affirmation at the right moment in a child's life and it's like lighting up a whole roomful of possibilities."
>
> —Gary Smalley

Zoe was so excited to head to preschool. She'd seen all the big kids get backpacks and lunch boxes. It was her time to carry her own lunch box, and she couldn't wait to help fill it up. Every single day, she wanted a cheese quesadilla and that was it! Her mom was getting frustrated and did everything she could to get her to try something different, but cheese quesadillas were her favorite. After two weeks of cheese quesadillas, her mom decided to get Zoe in the kitchen for a little exploration. They made different types of quesadillas, cheese and fruit kebabs, and crackers sandwiches. She and Zoe had a fun new list of lunch box foods. Mom also stopped asking her what she wanted for lunch each morning because she remembered that part of her role was to decide the *what*. She now had a new list of fun foods Zoe liked and packed accordingly.

Time to Fly

By now, your little one has moved into eating almost all foods or at least all textures foods can come in, with the exceptions of obvious choking hazards, like nuts, popcorn, and marshmallows. She can now use an open cup, sip from a straw, scoop with a spoon, and handle a fork. You may even brave the notion of helping your little one use a butter knife or child-safe knife with meals. Don't be shocked! Children all over the world learn how to use knives at an early age. As with everything, practice and a safe setting make for the best ways to learn. It's time. She has her wings, it's time to let her soar. Figuratively speaking, of course!

In addition to her soaring through her skills with utensils, she most likely has most of her teeth. Having a full set of choppers greatly improves her chewing capabilities and can give her more confidence when taking bites. But she may still try to bite off more than she can chew (don't we all?). Even while using her silverware and open cup and chomping down on her steak, there are still skills that need to be safely practiced and monitored. At this point, your little one may:

- Eat the same foods as the rest of the family
- Feed herself well with a spoon and fork
- Have definite food likes and dislikes
- Refuse certain foods or can become more picky
- Wipe her own mouth and hands with a napkin or cloth
- Start to serve herself at the table with minor spills
- Pour liquids into her cup from a small container

If these skills seem far from where your little one is right now, it's okay. Some little ones need a bit more encouragement and practice before they're ready to be an advanced eater. All children develop differently on their own timeline, and don't forget that time-based milestones are generalizations.

Is Little One Ready to Move On?

Let's look and see if your little one is ready to move into advanced eating.

Isla used an open cup and silverware when she enjoyed her mini hamburger, salad, and chocolate banana smoothie at dinner. She enjoyed showing off her skills of eating and drinking like her parents.

- ✔ Ready, Isla is eating and drinking well using her utensils and cup.
- ❑ Not Ready

Jack loved picking out his own snacks. When mom said it was snack time, he was able to open the snack drawer and pick out some crackers. He asked his mom for cheese to complete his afternoon snack. He knew he needed to ask for help when necessary.

- ✔ Ready, Jack is asking for help and making choices based on the options Mom is providing.
- ❑ Not Ready

Audrey struggled eating her soup and got frustrated with her meal. She wanted to use her spoon, but the soup kept getting all over her shirt instead.

- ❑ Ready
- ✔ Not Ready, Audrey may still need some help with a bigger, little-kid-friendly spoon with lots of praise at each try.

The Advanced Eater Safety Checklist

Although your little one is growing leaps and bounds and acting less like a toddler and more like a little girl ready to soar, there are still things we must continue to do to make the eating table a safe zone.

1. Toddler continues to eat at the table in high chair, booster seat supported with a foot rest, or toddler chair and is not walking around or eating while playing.

2. Distractions continue to be removed. Continue to foster the habit of being mindful during mealtimes.

3. Continue to stay present with your little one while eating.

4. Continue to test the temperature of cooked and mixed meals to make sure they're not too hot for her to handle, and encourage her to test the food and blow on it if needed.

5. Continue to provide appropriately sized pieces of food and coach child while chewing or offer to cut smaller when you see her struggling.

6. Continue to advance previously avoided foods and cut round foods in half lengthwise.

7. Continue to modify the texture as needed based on your little one's comfort level.

Nutrients to Consider

Growth and development may slow after infancy, but your little one still has a need for many nutrients via her nutritional intake. Your little one may be experiencing a lot of changes within her second and third years. If you're a parent, you're probably excited to refer to her as a two- or three-year-old instead of counting all the months! If your little one has started a daycare or preschool, or she is experiencing longer times away from home, you may notice that her eating patterns vary when she's is away. This is often a time when toddlers can experience changes in food preferences, hydration issues, and even experience constipation.

> **"Having a two-year-old is like having a blender you don't have the top for."**
> —Jerry Seinfeld

At this age, busy is the name of the game. Stop to drink? Stop to potty? Or go in a strange potty? Those are all legitimate concerns and considerations of a two-and-half-year-old. That's right! We even have to engage in potty talk to get an understanding of what's going on with our little ones, especially if they're away during the day. While some may not consider potty talk part of nutrition, it can provide a lot of important information. We can ask questions like when did she poo at school, did she have one today, did it hurt? These questions can tell us if she's holding back and not going potty when needed or if she's not well-hydrated. There's a reason why dietitians have lots of potty talks, even with grown-ups. When we ask you *how's it going*, you're going to think twice about what we mean. When we're asking about kids, we're looking for information that tells us if your little one is getting enough food, fiber, and/or water from day to day.

In addition to fiber and water needs, there are some additional nutrients that children in the United States often lack, such as calcium and potassium. With a focused intake of fruits and vegetables, with fewer overly processed foods, nutrient deficiencies like these shouldn't be an issue.

FIBER

There's a good chance your little one is pottying just fine with all the whole foods she's eating, but just in case she experiences constipation, let's look at fiber needs for toddlers. According to the Academy of American Pediatrics, children two and older should take in 5 grams of dietary fiber plus their age.[1] So if she is two or three, she should eat about 7 to 8 grams per day and up to 17 to 18 grams per day. If you're providing plenty of fruits and veggies, it's likely she's getting enough. You do not need to plan to hit the high end of fiber every day or count up the grams (please don't). Too much fiber can also cause issues like bloating, gas, diarrhea, and with too little water, even constipation. This is true for us adults, too.

Parents often take note of fiber needs when their toddler is being potty trained. If your little one has an adequate amount of fiber in her diet, her poo will be better formed and will likely have an easier exit on the potty. Having a little one strain on the potty is not an enjoyable process. High-fiber foods include all berries, beans, broccoli, cabbage, peas, nuts, and potatoes with their skin. Before you open up a box of twig-like cereal or opt for a fiber supplement, try a daily dose of blackberries or raspberries. One cup of berries has a whopping 8 grams of fiber, and it's a super tasty fiber vehicle. We don't believe that you have to buy a bunch of fiber-spiked foods to get enough fiber. It can be done the old-fashioned way, with fruits and veggies.

WATER

When taking in enough fiber, it's equally important to stay hydrated. Fiber takes up fluid to help it form and exit our bodies. Toddlers and preschoolers are active little beings. With their high activity levels from running, jumping, swinging, sliding, and constant playing comes an increased need of fluids. According to the Institute of Medicine's

Dietary Reference Intakes for Electrolytes and Water, the Adequate Intake (AI) for water for children aged one to three is 1.3 liters per day. That's about 44 fluid ounces, or roughly five and a half 8-ounce cups of water. Water is the beverage of choice for a toddler and preschooler. This is followed by milk (up to three 8-ounce cups per day) and, if desired, up to 4 ounces of 100 percent fruit juice per day. In addition to water, milk, and juice, some of your little one's fluid needs can be met with soups, yogurts, juicy fruits, and vegetables. Water can be obtained in a variety of ways, not just water consumption.

Toddlers often lack the ability to know they're thirsty or often forget to slow down to drink. If you find her urine is a dark yellow or is very strong smelling when she uses the potty then it's time to ramp up her fluids. Add fresh fruit to her water, make fruit ice cubes, add a splash of fruit juice, or make her some herbal tea like chamomile to help encourage her to drink water more frequently throughout the day. There are safe teas that are just for little ones these days. Who knew? Wendy Jo and Miss A have nighttime tea together. But don't forget that much like food, fluid needs can vary from child to child. Some need more and some need less. Some can even drink more than we do!

Calcium

The bone-building mineral, calcium, is a key nutrient for both babies and toddlers. Most think of bones when they refer to calcium, but it actually plays an important role in muscle contraction, nerve responses, enzymes, and hormone responses. Having a deficiency in calcium can equate to the body taking what it needs from bone. This can spell trouble for a toddler with growing and developing bones. Although milk has long received the fame as a source of calcium, other excellent sources can be included in the diet, as well. Almonds, yogurt, kefir, cheese, calcium-fortified orange juice, white beans, collard greens, and broccoli all provide some calcium. A child who drinks at least 2½ cups of milk per day is getting in enough calcium in a day. Breast milk has less than a third of the calcium that whole milk contains so, if breastmilk is still your toddler's drink of choice, look to add in yogurt, cheese, almonds, and greens throughout the day. But don't forget about that sunshine vitamin, vitamin D. Vitamin D is needed for calcium absorption. It's likely you're still supplementing with vitamin D since it's hard to get enough in food (this is true for little ones and their adults). Leslie gives CC a probiotic (which she calls her *pro-body-otic*) that also contains vitamin D each day.

POTASSIUM

A diet rich in whole, fresh fruits and vegetables will cover a toddler's needs of potassium, but if you're concerned that your little one is not getting enough, there's nothing wrong with a multiple vitamin and mineral daily supplement. Potassium plays an important role in blood pressure regulation, muscle functions, and heart contractions. A toddler who is deficient in potassium can seem fatigued, much like with iron deficiency. Potassium is found in most fresh fruits and vegetables with excellent sources being roasted potatoes, dried apricots, bananas, raisins, sunflower seeds, lima beans, almonds, and acorn squash. If your little one has a mostly balanced plate, then this nutrient won't be a concern unless underlying conditions are present.

Balanced Plate and Weight

A balanced plate, frequent offerings of fresh fruits and vegetables, and accessibility to healthy snacks will encourage your little one to start making smart decisions in fueling their bodies during play and rest. Leslie and Wendy Jo both talk about power foods and energy-giving foods with their girls, and finishing all their food is never a requirement. The *Born to Eat* team doesn't promote the *clean plate club*. Leslie jokingly says it took her almost twenty years to unlearn the not-so-mindful habits of the clean plate club. There's more truth to that than joke.

The American Academy of Pediatrics reminds physicians and parents that children have an innate ability to self-regulate their food intake at this age. The AAP cautions parents that these three practices are associated with excess weight gain in toddlers:

- feeding in response to emotional distress,
- using food as a reward, and
- excessive prompting or encouragement to eat.

It's tempting to prompt or encourage your child to eat more, take one more bite, or finish their plate. We get those urges, too! It's how many of us were raised, and we know our parents did the best they could with the information they had at the time. If you're ever in doubt, think back to Ellyn Satter's Division of Responsibility. As parents, we are responsible for *what* they are offered to eat, *when* they eat, and *where* they eat. Our little ones are in charge of *if* they eat and *how much* they eat. They can develop the best little bodies possible without a hyper-focus on food or weight. And remember, weight (like the BMI) is not a good indicator of health and should not be discussed with children.

Shake It Up

Before you say, "one more bite" or "come on, you can eat more" when you find your toddler falling into a food rut, let us reassure you, they are normal. Food jags, or when a child only wants a certain food or foods, normally only last a few weeks. Kids often get fixated on one food or another for a bit of time and then can quickly shift out of it or onto another food. Instead of focusing just on their food intake or encouraging them to have another bite, try shaking things up a bit. The joke about toddlers hating all the foods they loved yesterday can be oh so true.

If we don't make food a big deal, it likely won't end up being a big deal. When we engage in food fights or become a short-order cook, we could be inviting more struggles. There are things you can try that may help when you find your toddler refusing foods—even if it was a favorite yesterday. Changing up the texture, preparing the food with different spices, adding a sauce, putting it on a pizza, stuffing it into a quesadilla, adding into a soup, or topping it with cheese can be the small tweak needed to make a food more appealing to a free-thinking toddler. We've even found that simply changing what we call a food can work as well. Power-muscle sounds a lot more interesting and fun compared to steak, pork chop, or chicken thigh. Menu developers in restaurants do the same thing!

Try shaking up the texture or look of these common foods:	
Eggs	Boiled, scrambled, cheesy, egg salad, deviled eggs, egg muffin, frittata, quiche, or omelet
Meats	Steak finger, ground, chopped, in sauce, burgers, meatballs, meat muffin cups, kebabs, chili, or stew
Beans	Refried, hummus or dip, soup, added to quesadillas, bean patties (falafel), or mixed with ground meat in sauce
Greens	Salad, sautéed with garlic, chopped in scrambled eggs, chopped into burgers or meatballs, added into sauces, or smoothies
Fruit	Sliced, fruit stacks or kebabs, mixed in yogurt, baked, or mixed in oats

We don't believe in hiding foods or being dishonest with your little one. Empower her to help you in the kitchen and work with the different textures and preparation methods of foods. Even if she chooses not to taste or eat what she makes, it helps that she played with the food and learned new skills in the kitchen. Remember, picky eating or the occasional food jag is normal at times. If you feel that you have an extreme picky eater on your hands, refer back to Dr. Rowell's suggestions in chapter 8.

Are You Really Going to Eat That?

These can be trying times as parents, we know! As dietitians, we often hear comments like, "You let your kid eat that?" How we'd like to respond is, "It's rude to comment on my food or my kid's food and it's really not your business," but we refrain . . . usually. Most of the time, we tend to say, "We believe variety and balance are important for little eaters." Now remember, we're whole food, real food kind of gals, but we eat foods across the gamut and even overly processed foods at times. Heck, we even have some in our pantries. Time and time again in our counseling offices, we get the question about having certain foods in the house. Parents ask us if they should just keep those certain foods out of the house all together. Unless your child or family member has a food allergy, the answer is no and this is why.

Leslie uses this example over and over in her office. It's an example, but one she's witnessed in person many times. Two upset parents sit down in Leslie's office to discuss their family food choices but mainly those of little Johnny, who is now three years old. They give Leslie some background information about foods in their home and then they tell her what happened last week at a friend's party. Little Johnny isn't allowed to have chips or cookies at home. His parents feel like they're poor choices and have decided not to allow them in the home. They, his parents, are the nutritional gatekeepers of the home. However, little Johnny gets invited to a birthday party and chips and cookies are present. Little Johnny eats as much as he can until he feels sick from overeating. His parents have told him what a poor choice he made in eating those items and that it's unhealthy. They were very upset with him and thought they could use some help navigating food selections. That's why they're sitting in Leslie's office without little Johnny.

Leslie and little Johnny's parents talk about their roles as food providers and little Johnny's role as an eater. They discuss that yes, some foods are overly processed and do not possess the best nutrition quality. While those aren't foods we want to eat all the time, we need to learn how to deal with them when they're placed in front of us. If little Johnny felt like those foods were off-limits or taboo, it's very likely that he'll overdo it when given the opportunity. *When food is a big deal, it's a big deal!* Leslie and his parents developed a plan to incorporate those foods in their weekly menus. Leslie suggested they not mention anything about them being on his plate or in his lunch box. She also suggested that they

> "What you tell your kids about eating and weight can affect them the rest of their lives. Think well-being, not weight."
> —Marsha Hudnall, MS, RDN, CD

be part of a meal without some sort of special name and not something that comes afterward like *dessert*. This would allow little Johnny to self-regulate versus eating a meal just to get to his cookies and possibly overeat them. They, as the nutritional gatekeepers, learned that he could be trusted with those foods, and when they didn't make the food a big deal, it became less of desirable, or special, food for him. At first, he ate them all and ate them first. But, over time, little Johnny would even leave part of the cookie on his plate at dinner. The cookie was no longer a big deal.

Mini Burger
Cherry Tomatoes
Cookie

We, as nutritional gatekeepers, have the very important job of providing a variety of foods, even those we'd rather our kids eat less often. As we've mentioned before, the *how* we eat at this stage in life may very well be as important as the *what*. The *what* comes in time. If they know they can trust their bodies, and that you do too, they're more likely to be adventurous with foods of all kinds later on.

> As *Born to Eat* parents, we not only get to provide a variety of foods to our kids, but we have the pleasure and opportunity to teach them how to deal with all foods, regardless of their nutritional quality, in a healthy way.

Variety and Exploration

Variety and exploration starts at home and continues during the childhood experience. One of the most common variety experiences, or challenges, can be when your little one starts daycare or preschool at this age. We've both experienced packing lunches and snacks for time away from home. These are a few of our favorite go-to options.

Morning Snack	Lunch	Afternoon Snack
Orange Cottage Cheese Muffin (pg 187)	ham & cheese quesadilla + strawberry & blueberry skewers (on straws) + cherry tomatoes	almond butter topped crackers + dried apricots
pretzels	parfait with greek yogurt, granola, and berries	cheese stick + cherry tomatoes
banana + peanut butter	nacho tortilla chips with beef & melted cheese + sliced avocado	plain greek yogurt + sliced fruit
greek yogurt + frozen fruit smoothie	Avocado Chicken Salad (pg 195) wrap + carrot sticks	trail mix
applesauce	turkey apple sandwich squares + snap peas	cookie + milk

If you're worried that daycare or preschool personnel may not support your child's ability to self-regulate and use the Division of Responsibility, try using a lunch box card from our friend, Dr. Katja Rowell, The Feeding Doctor. She suggests that if someone asks your child to eat certain foods, have your child hand over the card on page 113. Leslie uses this in CC's lunch box. Feel free to make copies of the card.

CHAPTER 9 REFERENCES

1. Christine L. Williams, Marguerite Bollella, Ernst L. Wynder, "A New Recommendation for Dietary Fiber in Childhood," *Pediatrics* 96 (5) (November 1995), accessed online August 4, 2016, http://pediatrics.aappublications.org/content/96/5/985.

Lunch Box Card

Dear Friend of_____,
Please allow _____ to decide how
much to eat, and in what order, from what
I have packed. Even if that means all
_____ eats for lunch is "dessert," or if
_____ starts with dessert. I trust that
_____ can rely on hunger and
fullness signals to know how much to eat.
Please call my cell _____ if you
have any questions. The nice thing is,
this should be less work for you. If _____
needs help opening containers, I thank
you for that help, otherwise,
_____ should be good to go.
Thank you for all you do for our children.

Used with permission by Katja Rowell, MD, from
her 2012 book, *Love Me, Feed Me.*

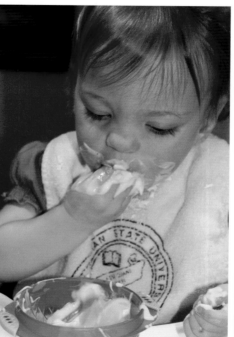

PART 3

THE *BORN TO EAT* FAMILY

Born to Eat isn't just a way of fostering a self-feeding or self-regulating child; it's a philosophy. We believe that having a healthy relationship with food starts at home even if you didn't grow up that way. The *Born to Eat* approach starts with baby but must be fostered in the family environment with supporting body trust, embracing different body types, finding pleasure in eating, taking care of ourselves, and planning for meals as a family. We believe we are all *Born to Eat*, not just our kids. We'll show you how to embrace it in this part of the book.

> "When you support your body, eat based on hunger and appetite, and acknowledge pleasure, you are more likely to maintain a stable body weight and enjoy improved nutrition—and to pass those values and skills on to your children."
>
> —Katja Rowell, MD

CHAPTER 10

IT'S A FAMILY AFFAIR

> "We cannot solve our problems with the same thinking we used when we created them."
> —Albert Einstein

Kelly didn't trust herself with food. She was pretty sure her mom didn't either. When she was younger, her mom would hide food from her. At first, she didn't notice, but then it became a trend. She'd remember being with her at the grocery store when they bought the chips and crackers together, but when she went to grab a snack, they weren't there. One day she found the chips. Not in a normal place to store food but an obscure spot that could only be a hiding spot.

As an adult, she realized her mom could have been hiding the chips from her just so she could get some for herself. But she sure didn't hide the apples. When she was young, Kelly interpreted this as a sign that she wasn't to be trusted with food and, in turn, she couldn't trust her own body. Something must've been wrong with her. As Kelly became an adult, she struggled with self-regulation and body trust. She moved from one diet to another until she realized dieting wasn't the answer. Kelly began working with a helping professional that supported her through the realization of how that experience had impacted her eating behaviors and body trust. She had carried so much shame about not being able to be trusted with food and had based many of her health and body choices on this experience.

Regardless of the initial intention of the hidden or restricted food, it had left a mark on her life. But she realized it didn't have to remain that way. Kelly was ready to truly take care of herself and that meant letting go of dieting, dieting tools, diet food, and those who didn't support her body confidence. She realized that trusting her body, practicing self-care, and combatting the negative voice in her head would take some work. This may have impacted her life, but she wasn't going to let it do the same in her daughter's life. She knew that dieting, restricting, or demonizing food in any way at home could undermine self-regulation and body trust for everyone under her roof. *Body distrust and body hatred are learned.* Kelly was going to do what she could to make her home a safe zone.

> We grew up in a time when dieting was routinely recommended by health professionals and considered healthy. Even though many still recommend dieting as a means to health, we now know better. Our children don't have to have the same experiences with dieting and body distrust. We can break the cycle with the *Born to Eat* approach.

This is just one story of how our development around food and eating can impact our lives, and subsequently our kids' lives. They're not all like this one. Some may be, yet so many of us have wonderful family influences but may have been negatively impacted by the predatory marketing of the dieting and weight-loss industry. And then there's the media, and Photoshop, and now filters for everything. Think back to the days when the only thing we needed filtered was coffee—no calories to count, no nutrition labels to scratch our heads over, and no apps to obsessively track the aforementioned numbers that may not make a difference in our health at all. We ate plain ol' food (most of which didn't have labels), we didn't even know about calories, and we made it as a population. It's very likely that in those times, the self-regulation with food that was developed and fostered in infancy and through childhood led to self-regulating adults. They didn't have all the numbers getting in the way of listening to their bodies.

> "With the research we have to date, it's not ethical to recommend any kind of dieting."
> —Evelyn Tribole, MS, RD, and coauthor of *Intuitive Eating*

In our dieting-obsessed culture, few people make it to adulthood trusting their bodies. Today, there's a lot of background noise telling us to eat this, or eat that, now don't eat that, okay now you can have that but only if it's clean (whatever that means), organic, and

> *Born to Eat* kids need *Born to Eat* parents!

passed through a filter of solid gold (slight exaggeration). No wonder it's hard to feel like we're feeding ourselves well out there with all the background noise that may or may not be coupled with our own issues with feeding development and eating behavior. But, there is hope. And thank goodness we are *what you chew is up to you* kind of people!

> If a weight-loss or diet program suggests that you sign up for the rest of your life, hold your wallet and run. Run really, really fast. It's a good idea to *avoid dieting altogether*. Dieting is a predictor of becoming overweight and a risk factor for developing binge-eating disorder.

With our collective experiences, we've been counseling adults, families, and age-appropriate children for about thirty years. In that time, we've found that *it is possible* to regain self-regulation and body trust, and do so while living in a dieting culture. The clients we've had the privilege to work with have taught us so much. While they're all so very different in the lives they lead, they all have one thing in common: they felt too busy and overwhelmed to take steps toward health that weren't in the form of diets. In fact, we realized that they didn't even know there *was* something else. We like to think "be reasonable and listen to your body" is a very sexy message, but it just hasn't made it to the mainstream.

How do we even start to listen to our bodies and trust them again if we've been swayed by dieting? It's possible, because we are, all of us young and old, *Born to Eat*. We have what it takes. It just takes time to turn up the volume on our self-regulation that the dieting world may have put on mute. Now, we realize that not everyone is caught up in the shaming dieting world, and that is fantastic! However, many are and it's affecting our health and happiness not just as individuals, but as families, too.

> This is a family affair, and there's no better time to create a whole family of self-regulating and body-trusting humans than when you're teaching your little one to do the same.

Like many of our clients, we feel too busy for self-care or self-observation at times. But without the self-observation of how our own feeding development and eating behaviors have impacted us, we don't even know where to start. This is the only way to find out what self-care may look like for us individually. Nothing changes for good without some nonjudgmental observation around our own behaviors.

You, in addition to your little one, have to be a priority, and that isn't selfish. You read that right—self-care is *not* selfish. It's similar to the *put your oxygen mask on before helping others* warning on a flight. Actually, it's not just similar, it's exactly the same thing—take care of you so you can help the one next to you. But in this case, the mask is the investigation or observation of your own behaviors. Once you have that info (oxygen flowing), you can start helping yourself by knowing what type of self-care you need to feel refreshed and nourished. We all tend to operate better on a full tank, whether that's filled with nourishment, accepting help, planning a meal, going for a walk, reading a book, enjoying a friend's company, or simply getting enough rest.

> "When you practice taking care of your body, you feel better living in it." –Leslie

We've both worked with parents who came in frazzled about planning meals or being healthy as a family. Many times, we have to focus just on the parent sitting in front of us because that parent is likely the nutrition gatekeeper for the home. They decide what comes into the home, what is served, when it is served, how food is planned, and usually the definition of health for the family. If this parent, which we see time and time again, isn't taking care of their own needs, it's likely the whole family feels the impact. For example, if Dad generally grocery shops and cooks and he's having a rough time at work or is sick, the family may not have the food items they normally have or meals might not get planned. When we are taken care of, we take care of others even better.

> "If you were the caregiver of another person the way you care for yourself, would you be guilty of neglect?"
>
> —D. Estep

When we think of self-care as a choice, it makes many of the activities more doable. Like if you know you feel better after going on a walk and you remind yourself that you are choosing to invest in your mental and physical wellness, it feels a lot better than a mindset or self-talk like *I should go exercise*.

Here's another example: *I should pack a healthy lunch for tomorrow.* This sure sounds better and more likely to happen: *I'm going to take this leftover burger tomorrow with a side salad because I feel better all afternoon when I have a tasty lunch.* We usually don't get anywhere positive *shouldn' on ourselves.* We laugh, but oh how true.

Over the years, we've collected many self-care strategies our clients have found useful and we want to share them with you. Our clients come from all different walks of life and family situations. You may pick one or two that resonate with you and your needs. That's just fine.

Sample Self-Care Activities for Parents, Caregivers, or any Living Adults

- ❑ I aim for 7 to 8 hours of sleep
- ❑ I get up 15 to 30 minutes early to read, pray, or journal
- ❑ I walk the dog and enjoy a beautiful day
- ❑ I plan and pack lunch the night before
- ❑ I plan evening meals or get help with planning
- ❑ I make a grocery list at least once a week and shop for groceries at least once a week
- ❑ I meet friends once a week for coffee or happy hour
- ❑ I use deep breathing or meditation exercises when anxious at home or work
- ❑ I ask for help with cooking, cleaning, or running errands
- ❑ I avoid dieting behaviors like skipping meals, restricting my energy intake, or using diet foods
- ❑ I let my body be my guide for hunger and fullness
- ❑ I avoid focusing on numbers like calories or weight
- ❑ I ignore or block those who make me second-guess my own body trust
- ❑ I share the joys and struggles with other parents or friends I trust
- ❑ I call a friend at a scheduled time each week
- ❑ I listen to my favorite play list while taking a walk
- ❑ I schedule movement or rest time in my schedule (so it actually exists)
- ❑ I carry a water bottle with me daily to stay hydrated
- ❑ I set my phone alarm for a self-care check-in and ask "How am I doing?" and "What do I need?"
- ❑ I'm aware of negative self-talk (the inner critic) and attempt to change that dialogue. For example, *I'm so awful at this baby-led weaning stuff, my kid deserves better* (um, that's harsh) is the inner critic. *Hang in there, this is new for both of us and we'll catch on soon* is more supportive and useful mental chatter. I can *choose* to change it.

If we're able to help Mom, Dad, or Uncle Joe see the impact their own self-care has on the family, we're making some great progress for everyone. Self-care isn't selfish. Take a moment right now to think about things you need as an individual, a parent, a caregiver, a friend, a coworker, or a nutritional gatekeeper. We hope these examples will get you thinking about your own needs and situation.

> "Daring to set boundaries is about having the courage to love ourselves, even when we risk disappointing others."
>
> —Brené Brown

Breaking the Dieting Mold

Many of our adult clients have worried about their own developmental issues around food and eating and how they might overcome the wounds or stronghold of their pasts. We have the pleasure of working one-on-one with them to move toward a healthier mindset around food and body. If you're one of those people or just want some great help in the direction of body trust, these are some of our favorite recommendations or self-care steps.

These are our favorite resources for adults wanting to regain body trust and buck the diet culture.

❏ *Intuitive Eating*, written by nutrition experts Evelyn Tribole and Elyse Resch

❏ *Daring Greatly: How the Courage to Be Vulnerable Transforms the Way We Live, Love, Parent, and Lead*, written by Brené Brown, PhD (we love all of her books)

It starts with slowing down enough and decreasing distractions so we can listen to our own body cues. This means setting boundaries around time so that we have the head space to ask ourselves some questions about what we might need. Am I hungry? Thirsty? Full? We so often just eat by the clock or eat all the items we plugged in on our tracker app. Eating by the time or by a caloric amount doesn't set us up to self-regulate. If we can take the time to wait and act on hunger, it's a step in the right direction. It is possible to trust the body again after years of dieting—we've seen it happen time and time again—but it takes patience and trust that the body will do what it's meant to do. The body is capable of giving you physical cues to eat, helping you feel when you're satisfied so that you can stop eating when you've had enough. We're capable of eating both intuitive and intelligently. If we're used to quantifying things and want to know how much to eat if we're not counting something, we can try this.

The Hunger and Fullness Gauge can help us learn our cues if we're not in the habit of paying attention to them or not used to allowing self-regulation. Before we start to eat, we can try to identify where we fall on the hunger side of the scale. As we're eating, and taking our time, we can see how it moves from hungry, to satisfied, to comfortably full. And, sometimes, self-regulating, normal eaters hit the too full mark—like *every* time Leslie goes to a Mexican restaurant—and that's okay.

Using Your Own Gauge for Hunger and Fullness

Think of fueling your body like fueling your car. If there's no gas, it goes nowhere. The body is a complex machine that needs to be fueled several times per day to keep you satisfied and moving efficiently. It'd be nice, but the body doesn't have an external gauge posted to show you when to eat or stop eating. We must re-learn how to feel our body's internal gauge, or self-regulation, at work. It starts with one question: "Am I physically hungry?"

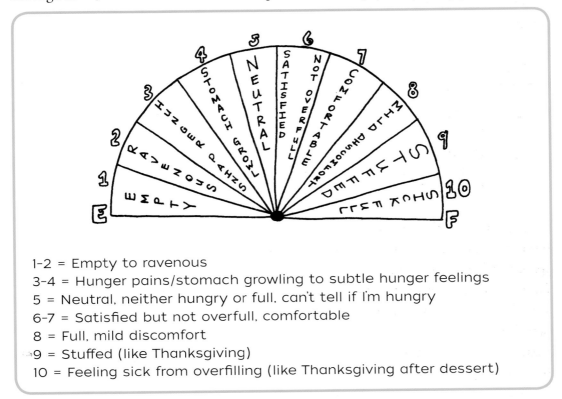

1-2 = Empty to ravenous
3-4 = Hunger pains/stomach growling to subtle hunger feelings
5 = Neutral, neither hungry or full, can't tell if I'm hungry
6-7 = Satisfied but not overfull, comfortable
8 = Full, mild discomfort
9 = Stuffed (like Thanksgiving)
10 = Feeling sick from overfilling (like Thanksgiving after dessert)

At first, you may want to keep a food journal and note how you felt before and after an eating opportunity (meal or snack). You can skip all the numbers, like calories and grams of stuff. That information doesn't help you determine hunger or fullness. First, determine where you fall on the gauge before you eat a meal or snack. Then take a moment during the meal or snack to ask yourself how the food tastes and if your satisfaction level is beginning to change. Do you need a little more or are you starting to feel comfortable and satisfied? When you finish eating, use the scale to determine where you fall after the meal or snack. It could be just right (a 6 to 7), not enough (a 4 to 5), or too much (an 8 to 10). Remember that self-regulating eaters sometimes get too little food (darn, I left my lunch at home and made do) and sometimes get too much (once slice of pizza too many). That's normal from time to time and gives you experience for points of reference. And last but not least, re-learning to be a self-regulating and intuitive eater takes practice and patience.

10 Ways *Born to Eat* Parents Can Support Body Trust in *Born to Eat* Kids

1. Talk about listening to and honoring our bodies. For example, if you're hungry, you're honoring your body by eating. If you're full, you're honoring your body by stopping. If you're tired, you're honoring your body by going to bed. If you're eating a food and decide it's not that good, you're honoring your body by not eating something you find isn't satisfying.

2. Compliment each other on things that aren't related to looks or weight. For example, "Miss A, you must really be using your learning skills, your ABCs are great!" Or, "CC you ran so fast in the yard, you must be getting great energy!" It's okay to say a child is cute, pretty, or handsome, but they need to know they're so much more like strong, courageous, smart, caring, capable, etc.

3. Discuss all the amazing things our bodies can do like run, jump, hug, learn, and get energy from the foods we eat.

4. Do not talk negatively about your own body. You are their most beautiful example, regardless of how you feel about your body–own it.

5. Do not talk negatively about others' bodies. Ever. Redirect negative talk about others.

6. Embrace our own unique differences from body shape to food preferences. Some people live in smaller bodies while others live in larger bodies. Some people like asparagus and some people don't.

7. Take care of yourself and have fun. It's the best example a child can have of living a healthy and happy life.

8. Never allow name-calling, especially those referring to one's body, ways of eating, or uniqueness. Stigma around differences in things like weight or looks are learned. They don't have to be.

9. Talk about your own preferences around food and taking care of your body while being open to trying new foods and activities.

10. Make living a healthy and happy lifestyle a family affair.

New Parent Stress

There are many joys of being a new parent. We often joke with our friends about all the not-so-joyous stuff that people forgot to tell us. Most of us know that we'll suffer from sleep deprivation, but have no idea what that actually feels like until a month or two after baby is born. In baby's first year, parents will accumulate a 350-hour sleep deficit.[1] That's about two weeks of lost sleep. Lost sleep can cause many other problems like eating too much, eating too little, becoming depressed, being a sleepy driver, being the parent with the short temper (been there), and the list goes on. When we aren't well-rested, we often look for something to eat or drink to combat fatigue and increase alertness. Sleep deprivation also impacts cognition and disease states and can lead to premature aging. But these are things we might expect.

It's what we don't expect that causes problems. Big ones. The kind that result in neglect. Now we're not suggesting that you would neglect your little one; we're suggesting that, like most parents, you'd neglect yourself to make sure that didn't happen. And we do that, until we can't do it any longer. This is why it's especially important for new parents to make a habit of self-care a priority, whatever that looks like for you.

CHAPTER 10 REFERENCES

1. Karisa Ding, "Sleep Deprivation and New Parents," *HealthDay* (January 20, 2016), date accessed September 20, 2016, https://consumer.healthday.com/encyclopedia/parenting-31/parenting-health-news-525/sleep-deprivation-and-new-parents-643886.html.

CHAPTER 11

WHAT YOU CHEW IS UP TO YOU—CHOOSING FOODS FOR YOUR FAMILY

> "Don't define your world in black and white. Because there is so much hiding amongst the grays."
>
> —Unknown

CC was just over a year old when she visited Wisconsin for the first time. Leslie and her husband were excited for her to meet friends, relatives, and Aunt Bonnie's cows. CC had been self-feeding for about nine months now. She loved exploring her food and playing with it on her plate before she crammed it into her mouth. This was her first experience seeing food where it began: in the garden and on the farm. Aunt Bonnie and the cousins were excited to show her the garden. CC went straight for the tomatoes. She picked one right off the vine and shoved into her mouth. At that moment, Leslie realized what an amazing experience this was for her daughter. She got to see a tomato at its freshest moment, not in a package at the grocery store, but right out of the dirt. Just a few miles down the road at Grandma and Grandpa's house, she got to eat an apple right off the tree, along with cucumbers, carrots, rhubarb, and raspberries in the garden. Leslie realized just how important this experience was—not everyone gets to see where their food *really* comes from.

Everyone's An Expert

These days, everyone's an expert. Someone seems to always be telling us what we should do, from where to buy our food, how it should be grown, how to serve it, and what to abstain from. It's exhausting for consumers and infuriating for many nutrition professionals. The misinformation and useless recommendations run rampant. It's hard to know who to believe when it comes to nutrition advice, especially since it seems to change every day. Not only does everyone have an opinion, but they're adamant about it! With social media in the mix, posting real-time food and nutrition information, it can make feeding our little ones confidently a challenge, or at the very least, extremely frustrating.

Even as dietitians, we sometimes find ourselves sifting through the nonsense and evaluating the details to divvy up the facts from the fiction to make informed decisions. Daily, we can get sucked into posts that can make us question foods or certain ingredients. Could x, y, z be linked to this, that, and the other, and if we eat it, will we gain a third eye (insert sarcasm)? We all want what is best for our children, and social media makes it hard to know what a valid tip is, what a sales pitch is, or what is purely fear propaganda (sometimes finely veiled marketing). It's easy to fall victim to the random, fear-inspiring post. With that said, remember that you can filter out much of that static. Leslie likes to tell her clients to try to insert the *that does not necessarily apply to me* filter in their minds when they see nutrition information pop up on social media or in the mainstream media. It's very possible (and likely probable) that someone's interpretation of said *research* could be just plain wrong, may not even be legitimate research, and could send us down a dangerous path.

When you're not sure where to turn for this information, don't sweat it—we've got you covered. If you really want to do some extensive reading about the science surrounding questions like "What about genetically modified organisms (GMO)?" and "Do I need to eat fresh or frozen, organic or nonorganic?" and so on, Marion Nestle's book *What to Eat* would be a useful resource for you. But we're going to do our best to tackle some of these questions to help you in a quick, practical, and user-friendly way. No matter what, don't forget these seven words: *what you chew is up to you*. You get to make the choice about what you feel is best for you and your family based on the information you choose to absorb from people (or organizations) you choose to trust.

Let us be real with you: we both like to buy local when available, organic when it seems like a smart choice, and many day-to day conventional choices. We do the best we can with the information and resources we have (time, money, availability, etc.). We both agree: we aren't going to let this cause undue stress in our lives or cause our kids to worry about whether the food in front in them is organic. We (and our families) are very grateful that we have food in front of us. With that said, let's get started . . .

Organic, Conventional, or Natural?

Label	Organic Foods	Conventional Foods	Natural
Definition	Can only grow crops using organic-approved chemical pesticides or organic fertilizers, such as manure. Organic foods are non-GMO (genetically modified organisms).	Can use fertilizers, pesticides, and weed killers in the growing of crops. Can use GMO crops.	Currently, no developed definition. Any manufacturer can label their product as natural. It holds no value, nutritionally or otherwise.
Pros	The general ideology of organic farming practices are to conserve and preserve natural resources and reduce pollution. No synthetic pesticides and less overall pesticide residue.	Ability to grow a more consistent, fruitful, and abundant crop annually. Conventional growing meets the demands of an ever-growing population. Tends to be cheaper.	At this point, means nothing, so has no pros.
Cons	Most organic farms are much smaller in scale than their conventional counterparts and require greater efforts to maintain healthy crops. Large-scale operations still use conventional methods that are approved by USDA Organic standards. Organic foods are likely more expensive. Organic foods may have a *health halo*, giving the perception that it is always healthy—an organic cookie is still a cookie (not that we are opposed to cookies, but just sayin').	Potentially harms soil with heavy use of pesticides and fungicides. Bugs develop a resistance to chemicals used, making them more difficult to control or manage over time. Possible greater pesticide residue on conventional foods. Cross-contamination into organic farms.	At this point, means nothing, so has no cons. Arsenic (poison) is natural—don't go out of your way to eat it.

Our take on this heated debate is this: picking a side of organic or conventional is like saying there's a good and a bad way to farm. Based on the science, we enjoy, appreciate, and understand both ways of growing food. We recognize it's a growing world, and we want more people to eat fruits and vegetables, no matter which growing method may work best to fit a person's budget and their personal environmental decisions. We have both met with many conventional farmers working at making great strides toward reducing their environmental footprint and minimizing waste. We've also met the organic farmers and have seen their fully operating organic farms and innovative ways to utilize their resources. It's easy to get caught up in the debate, but you truly get a different perspective when you speak to the farmers or ranchers involved in growing our almonds, avocados, potatoes, grapes, dairy cows, beef cattle, and more. As for nutritional differences, this too is an ongoing debate in science, with one study suggesting nutritional superiority one day but none in the next study. It just depends on so many variables. It's enough to make a sane person crazy.

Stretching the Food Dollar

It's important to think about our food dollars and how we can make eating more whole foods feasible for the family budget. There are great whole foods that are cost-effective and nutritious. Don't forget about dried beans, frozen and canned foods, and weekly sale items. Some discount grocery stores offer produce, dairy items, meats, canned foods, frozen foods, and more for a budget-friendly price. Many farmers' markets accept payments from the Supplemental Nutrition Assistance Program (SNAP), as well.

One of us (not Leslie) is a big gardener. Wendy Jo has had the pleasure of living in many states throughout the United States and living abroad in Germany. While living in Texas and Virginia, Wendy Jo saw the need for products to help keep her crops alive or free from being chewed to death by predators. Whereas in California, she found she had few bugs to compete with and used very little to grow her citrus, pomegranates, figs, and vegetables. While in Germany, she could grow bountiful crops without ever using anything beyond manure (you don't want to eat that, either). Wendy Jo prefers to grow without pesticides and fungicides, and who wouldn't? She also wanted to protect her zucchini in Virginia without standing guard 24/7 to fight off garden invaders.

Wendy Jo's approach has always been to garden and seek to understand the climate and land she lives on and then go from there in growing foods for her family. She grows just for her family and cannot fathom the efforts it takes to grow and feed a nation as large as the United States. We love our local farmers and know they're out to earn an honest living, work hard to get food into our grocery stores, and (like the rest of us) want to feed their own families well. So, much like other debatable topics, there are many sides to this story. Get out there and meet your local purveyors and make a feasible decision based on where you live. What you chew is up to you!

Locally Sourced Foods

Let's be honest: between the two of us living in the land of year-round growing, sunny Southern California and Las Vegas, we may have a slight advantage over others when it comes to eating local year-round. Again, we're lucky and grateful for it. However, we've both lived all over the United States. We get it—local and fresh may seem best, but the reality is that this is not feasible or desirable all year long in many places in the United States. There are items that you can focus on getting locally, like dairy, meats, seasonal produce, and eggs.

Sometimes we can find great blueberries in the grocery or at the market, but other times they don't have a lot of flavor. We love blueberries and so do our families, so it's nice to have them year-round. If you're like us, you can embrace the flavor no matter the season by freezing those regional berries at their peak. Local produce, organic or not, is a great option for produce picked at their prime and delivering peak nutrition for that food. Blueberries don't grow everywhere, but when they're fresh, we want them. When we can't get them, we'll head on over to the freezer section and pick up some frozen blueberries. They're pretty tasty dried, as well. This is true for most produce, not just blueberries. It's a great idea to focus on locally available first.

Many people don't realize that local produce can deliver more nutrition. Yep, that's what we said. Local can be more nutritious because it has less transit time. If something is picked in the morning and you pick it up at the farmers' market that afternoon, that is *fresh*. This also means that the vegetable or fruit has had the least amount of time to be oxidized, exposed to light, and lose nutrients. A farmers' market doesn't just offer great local items; it's also a great experience for kids (and adults) to visit and talk to farmers. If you're unsure about this, check out the USDA's website www.localharvest. org to find nearby Community Supported Agriculture (CSA boxes), farmers' markets, and a great and often economical resource based on what's available in your area.

Keeping it Seasonal

Although we may love strawberries in December, and both of our little ones do, they won't be the sweetest and freshest produce at your local market. Shift gears toward what's in season to maximize the fruit and vegetables nutritional potential and maximum flavor. Let's be real, again: fresh *is* best when it's in season. It doesn't mean we're not going to pick up strawberries in the winter; it just means we're aware of this fact. We love quick-reference guides (we're card-carrying geeks and love it), so here's our handy-dandy seasonal chart.

Born to Eat Seasonal Vegetable Guide		
Spring to Summer	*Fall to Winter*	*Year-Round*
Artichokes	Broccoli	Arugula
Asparagus	Butternut squash	Beets
Bell peppers	Cauliflower	Carrots
Corn	Kale	Chard
Cucumbers	Lettuce	Mushrooms
Eggplant	Pumpkin	Spinach
Green beans	Sweet potatoes	
Peas		
Summer squashes		
Tomatoes		

Born to Eat Seasonal Fruit Guide		
Spring to Summer	*Fall to Winter*	*Year-Round*
Apricots	Apples	Apples
Blackberries	Figs	Avocado
Blueberries	Kiwi	Grapefruit
Cherries	Pears	Lemons
Melons	Plums	Limes
Nectarines	Pomegranates	Oranges
Peaches		
Pineapple		
Raspberries		
Strawberries		

Ways to Make the Most of Each Season

❏ Sign Up for a CSA (Community Supported Agriculture) Box if available in your area.

❏ Find and shop at a local farmers' market when available.

❏ Look through grocery store advertisements for seasonal deals on fruits and vegetables.

❏ Buy in bulk and freeze or can extras to enjoy all year long.

❏ Dry or make fruit leather (page 209) with your favorite seasonal fruit.

❏ Focus on recipes and meal planning that use seasonal produce.

❏ Grow your own! Lettuce, tomatoes, kale, and herbs are excellent plants for patio pots or on a windowsill.

Freezing and Buying Seasonal Produce

Whether it is an abundance of berries or a bumper crop of tomatoes, you can make your summer crops or farmers' market finds stretch throughout the year, if you're like Wendy Jo. To freeze berries, wash them and gently pat them dry. Once dry, place a nonstick silicone baking mat or piece of parchment paper down onto a jelly roll pan, then spread the berries out onto the pan in a single layer. If the berries are crowded, they'll stick together, so give them some room and keep it to a single layer. Place the pan into your freezer and freeze for at least 4 hours. Once frozen, place berries into a freezer-safe storage container, label, and freeze for up to 6 months or a year in a deep freezer.

Berries and most stone fruits (like peaches, plums, and nectarines) freeze relatively easily, whereas vegetables take a bit more effort. But they're well worth the effort! For green beans, carrots, and corn, simply blanch (toss into boiling water and boil for 3 minutes then immerse into an ice bath for 1 minute to halt the cooking) the vegetables then pat dry and freeze in the same manner you did with berries.

Tomatoes are probably one of the best vegetables (okay, yes, it's a fruit, but for the sake of preparation, we will call tomatoes a vegetable) to freeze, because who doesn't love the taste of a vine-ripened tomato? Yum. First, wash your tomatoes, and with a paring knife mark an X on the bottom of each tomato, gently piercing the skin. Next, pour boiling water over the tomatoes and let them sit for 1 minute. If you let them sit too long, they'll become mushy. Then place the tomatoes into an ice bath for 1 minute. You'll notice the skins are probably starting to peel off the tomatoes, so gently use your fingers to remove the rest of the skin. You can either freeze individually or toss into a freezer-safe bag and freeze in bulk for a tomato sauce or soup later in the winter.

Now, if you're like Leslie, you can pick up all of these in the freezer section of your local grocery—Leslie's definition of local (haha, she likes farmers' markets, too). We believe that frozen fruits and veggies you find in your grocery are a great option that is often overlooked. Frozen foods are picked, prepped, and packaged at peak season so that you can have great nutrition readily available anytime of the year. Speaking of freezing, don't be too quick to overlook your canned goods section of your local market. Where Wendy Jo may be the girl who actually cans her own bumper crop, you may be more like Leslie and opt for picking up your canned foods at the grocery store. If you have environmental or health concerns with canned goods, consider glass jarred canned foods, vegetable pouches, or non-BPA lined cans. Check out our favorite freezer and canned staples in chapter 13.

Keeping It Real

We believe in this motto: *Eat real food. Feel real good*™. We believe this so much that one of us (maybe Leslie) trademarked it! Over the years, we've realized that this "real" term really can irritate people. We're okay with that because we have our own definition of what real means to us (defined initially in the *Born to Eat* introduction). We believe keeping it real is about eating whole foods most of the time (meaning not diet food or overly processed food) and being able blend in pleasurable foods (cupcakes, obviously) regardless of their nutritional content and without worry. So now our motto is: *Eat real food, feel real good, but don't get crazy!* Truly. Don't make yourself crazy striving for organic, local, hormone-free, dye-free, and so forth. Make the choice that seems right for you and your family. Sometimes that's organic, sometimes it's dye-free, and sometimes it's plain ol' conventional food.

Can Healthy Eating Go Too Far?

You may or may not have heard of Orthorexia. It was first termed by Steven Bratman, MD. Orthorexia nervosa is not currently a clinical diagnosis, yet this unhealthy obsession of superior or righteous eating can lead to nutrient deficiencies, social isolation, and even a clinical diagnosis of an eating disorder. So yes, sometimes one's perception of healthy eating can go too far.

A perfect diet is simply impossible so balance is our best bet. Striving for perfection is not only not achievable, but it can make you feel crazy, and possibly set you up for disordered eating or chronic dieting. We both want to save you from this madness. Do yourself a favor and keep it real (within your reality) the best you can.

A Useful Shopping Guide

We both like to use, and recommend to our clients, a shopping guide called the *Dirty Dozen and Clean Fifteen* by the Environmental Working Group. This guide breaks down which foods have the most (dirty) or least (clean) pesticide residues.

Dirty Dozen

1. Strawberries
2. Apples
3. Nectarines
4. Peaches
5. Celery
6. Grapes
7. Cherries
8. Spinach
9. Tomatoes
10. Sweet Red Bell Peppers
11. Cherry Tomatoes
12. Cucumbers

Clean Fifteen

1. Avocado
2. Sweet Corn
3. Pineapple
4. Cabbage
5. Sweet Peas, frozen
6. Onions
7. Asparagus
8. Mangos
9. Papayas
10. Kiwi
11. Eggplant
12. Honeydew Melons
13. Grapefruit
14. Cantaloupe
15. Cauliflower

We don't always follow this to a *T* but it's a nice guide. These lists can help you decide when and if it's worth it to spend that five bucks on an apple. Be sure to check back for revisions on the guide each year because things change. Don't get crazy. Even if you don't stick to this list, you can still enjoy fruits and vegetables. It's about balance. Just give your fruits and vegetables a good scrub, or if you're very concerned, peel off the outer layer of skin on the fruits and vegetables that may be high on the dirty list. Wendy Jo does a 1:1 white vinegar and water solution on her produce to help clean the outer surfaces of the fruits and vegetables.

Life and food are about balance; so, instead of living in fear about eating conventionally grown produce or avoiding them all together, just think about eating more local and seasonal foods as often as you can. The bottom line is *what you chew is up to you*. Keep it real for you and your *Born to Eat* family. And don't forget that you get to make your own definition of *real* for your family.

> "It's all about #cleaneating, so I just wash every donut with soap before I take a bite. #Joking #DontDoThis #YesEvenWeEnjoyDonuts"
>
> —Wendy Jo

CHAPTER 12

FAMILY MEALS AND MEAL PLANNING

> "You don't have to cook fancy or complicated masterpieces, just good food from fresh ingredients."
>
> —Julia Child

It was the first day of school and it had been a busy day for the whole family. Jane was two years old and had just started preschool and Henry was five and started kindergarten. Elizabeth was exhausted from the last couple of days getting her kids ready for school and working on a project at work. Luckily, she'd remembered to get out the slow cooker over the weekend and planned to make chicken for tacos tonight. They got home and the main part of the meal, the salsa chicken, was done. It was a lifesaver after such a busy day.

It wasn't until they all sat down at dinner that they really had time to talk. Jane had met two new friends and was so excited about her round plate and triangle tortilla chip. Henry dug in and said the tacos were great and he was so hungry. He also mentioned that he was sad that a few of his pre-K buddies ended up in a different class. Elizabeth enjoyed dinner while talking to her kids about friendship and how wonderful it is to have friends—both old and new. The tacos were a hit while using much needed convenience (slow-cooked chicken), but the star of dinnertime was the connection to each other through conversation. The family meal is about so much more than food.

Family Meals and Meal Planning

Sharing a tasty meal with friends and family is always a treat, but research suggests that engaging in a family meal provides benefits far greater than physical nourishment. Consistently sitting down to family meals may reduce the likelihood of a child engaging in disordered eating behaviors and has been linked to less depressive symptoms.[1] This time spent together as a family may also make a child more likely to eat healthier foods and less likely to experience weight concerns. The benefits of the family meal don't stop there. As our kids get older, play sports, and have more homework, the family meal may be one of the few times of connection during a busy week. We may never know that our daughter's feelings got hurt at school if we didn't have that time to talk about it over tacos.

Over the years, we've worked with families that long for a family meal but just don't know how to make it happen within their reality. And, not every family looks the same or has a schedule that allows for consistent family meals. Some realities are just that—reality. Dad may commute an hour to work and not get home until 7:30, but the kids are starving by 6:00. The reality is that they can't wait on Dad for dinner, but Dad is always there making breakfast and sitting down to eat with the kids in the morning. Another family may have trouble getting all three kids ready for dinner at the same time every night, but they found a way to plan for Mom, Dad, and the three kids to secure family meal reservations every Tuesday, Thursday, and Sunday. Although dinner is the most common time for a family meal, there's no rule that says it has to be dinner. A family meal can be any meal (or snack if that's the time you have) during the day with at least one child and one parent (or any loved one) present.

> "Supper is about nourishment of all kinds."
>
> —Miriam Weinstein

If you and your family aren't in the habit of having family meals, it can be a challenge to get everyone on board at first. We've found these tools and tips helpful in our practices.

- ❏ Have kids help with dinner preparation like chopping or scooping.
- ❏ Have kids help set the table.
- ❏ Have kids decorate the table for the season or make placements.
- ❏ Place a jar on the table full of conversation starters, like who's your favorite actor, what's your favorite book, or what was the craziest thing you saw today?
- ❏ Go around the table and let everyone tell a joke.

❑ Let everyone share the highs and lows of the day. For example, today my high was going on a walk with my mom and my low was that I didn't get to play with my best friend.

❑ Go around the table and let everyone talk about one thing they're grateful for that day.

❑ Keep dinner talk positive. This is not the time for scolding about a bad grade or bad attitude with the kids. It's also a good idea to keep adult issues like an irritating coworker or financial concerns off the table.

❑ Ask each family member to stay at the table until everyone is finished (remember all that conditioning you do with a baby pays off later). If your toddler isn't particularly hungry and becoming a distraction for others, it's okay to let them leave the table as long as they don't disrupt the meal for others. Do what works best for your family.

❑ Remember that the words *you don't have to eat it* can calm a mealtime storm and help redirect with less struggle.

Slowing Down

Somewhere along the way, we've found ourselves rushing through meals, eating on the go, or approaching a drive-thru a window to pick up a quick bite on the way home from sports practice. Our self-induced craziness is not always loved, but it's often a reality in twenty-first century America. For Wendy Jo, moving overseas for her husband's job was a bit like going back in time. Where she lived, there was no fast food, most restaurants nearby were closed on Sundays and Mondays, and all grocery stores closed from Saturday at 1:00 p.m. until Monday at 8:00 a.m. If you happen to run out of eggs on Saturday or needed milk for Monday morning, you were out of luck. On the positive side, no one rushed patrons away from their dining table when eating out, bread breaks were a real thing and so were the afternoon cake breaks. Who wouldn't love a cake break?

Needless to say, Wendy Jo found that food isn't a big deal around Europe, meaning it isn't scrutinized, picked over, and served with lite dressing on the side. The food is real, wholesome, savored, and topped with butter. Wendy Jo will be the first to admit she missed some of the nice conveniences about the United States (especially when the aforementioned need of eggs or dairy arose at 6:00 p.m. on a Saturday evening), but she also began to appreciate how life slowed down, food wasn't demonized, and seasonal fruits and vegetables were truly appreciated. Without this experience, she may not have brushed up on her meal-planning skills as thoroughly. Wendy Jo realized that without meal planning and knowing how to cook the basics, moving abroad or even just living in a more rural area could be frustrating.

We can see how easy it could be to rely on conveniences like the drive-thru when a person doesn't know how to cook or meal plan. We get it, and we've been in drive-thrus here and there, too. Not everyone is a foodie or wants to be a chef, but we're guessing that by reading this book, you want to nourish your baby, and family, the best way you can. We're here to help empower you with kitchen essentials and meal-planning tips. In the chapters to follow, we will also touch on basic skills to becoming a better cook with simple recipes to help support your *Born to Eat* family. But first, let's get everything in its place.

Everything in Its Place

Our kitchens don't need to be five-star restaurants, but we can learn some great tips from those who've made cooking and serving great food their business. We feel that the French phrase *mise en place*, which means "everything in its place," can set the stage for an efficient and useful kitchen. In the restaurant world, chefs often refer to *mise en place* as the art of prepping items prior to starting to cook a dish or meal. In the real world of our home kitchens, this holds true, as well. Recall the times you've started to make cookies and realized you were short an egg. We'll admit it, even Wendy Jo with her culinary training has started mixing up a batch of cookies just to realize she was short that crucial ingredient. There is tremendous value to meal planning, grocery shopping accordingly, and then pre-prepping items to get yourself ready for the cooking the dish.

There's a reason why companies that deliver mostly prepared groceries accompanied by recipes have become popular in the United States. We like things in their place, and they take on the planning and prepping for us. All we have to do is chop and cook. Having everything in its place or *mise en place* is helpful for all of us. Let's start with our primary food storage areas.

Dry Goods, or the Pantry

Your dry goods are foods or ingredients that can hang out on the shelf for a bit of time, like canned goods, pasta, rice, grains, beans, spices, dried herbs, vinegars, nuts, nut butters, snacks like trail mix, nut and fruit bars, and whole-grain crackers. These items need to be stored in a cabinet or in a pantry.

Cold Storage, or the Fridge

Keep items like whole fat yogurts, whole milk, butter, cheeses, deli meats, berries, carrots, celery, citrus, nut butters, your favorite condiments, and seasonal greens stored in your fridge. Note: Keep your refrigerator clean and less full than you may think so airflow can deliver cold air to all of your foods, keeping your food safe and at the right temperature (below 40°F).

From the Freezer

Stock your freezer with meats, fish, poultry, nuts, staple vegetables and fruits, premade dinners, and convenience foods that help you out on the nights where dinner is rushed. Similar to the refrigerator, avoid overstuffing your freezer, as your foods won't stay as cold and may suffer from freezer burn when too full. Plus, it's harder to know what you have on hand if you can't quickly see what's stored in the freezer. Keep your freezer below 0°F.

Non-Fridge Perishable Storage, or the Fruit Bowl

Great fruits to keep on hand include apples, pears, bananas, oranges, kiwi, dried fruits, canned fruits, and fruit leather. Buy only what you can enjoy within a week to avoid food waste. Keep bananas separated from your fruit bowl, as the gases emitted from a banana can help ripen your other fruit too quickly. Having a colorful arrangement of fresh fruits available invites everyone to eat more fruits throughout the day. If it's in your eyesight, you'll remember you have it.

Born to Eat Staples			
Pantry	**Refrigerator**	**Freezer**	**Snack Basket**
Spices (salt, pepper, garlic powder, cumin, coriander, chili powder, cinnamon, turmeric, vanilla)	Milk	Steaks	Low-ingredient crackers
Dried herbs (thyme, rosemary, parsley, oregano)	Cheese, cheese sticks	Ground meats	Pretzels

Pantry	Refrigerator	Freezer	Snack Basket
Born to Eat Staples			
Oils (olive, coconut, canola, sesame)	Yogurts	Bacon	Fruit and nut bars
Vinegars (white, apple cider, red wine, balsamic, rice wine)	Deli meats	Whole chicken and chicken breasts	Trail mix
Soy sauce or Bragg's liquid aminos	Condiments (ketchup, mayonnaise, mustard, Worcestershire sauce, barbecue sauce, salad dressings, jams, pickles, olives, capers)	Frozen vegetables (broccoli, onion, peppers, corn, green beans, spinach)	Dried fruits with no added sugar like raisins or mango slices
Flours	Berries	Frozen fruits (berries, mangos, bananas, peaches, cherries)	
Sugars	Carrots	Pre-made dinners (lasagna, chicken pot pies, shepherd's pie)	
Leavening agents (baking powder, baking soda)	Celery	Convenience foods (frozen bread dough, pizzas, precut veggie blends, meat sauce)	
Grain or grain alternatives (rice, quinoa, couscous, oatmeal, etc.)	Citrus	Frozen seafood (shrimp, fish)	
Pasta	Apples		

Born to Eat Staples			
Pantry	**Refrigerator**	**Freezer**	**Snack Basket**
Canned goods (tomatoes, tomato paste, tomato sauce, beans, green beans, corn, etc.)	Nut butters		
Dried beans	Seasonal greens (lettuce, kale, Swiss chard, spinach, arugula)		
Shelf-stable vegetables (onions, shallots, garlic, potatoes, winter squash, sweet potatoes)	Butter		

We recommend keeping a fruit bowl out on the counters. It doesn't hurt to keep veggies out too—it helps us remember to cook them! All other foods should be stored out of sight in dry or cold storage. This helps us let our bodies give us cues to eat instead of a snack on the counter visually stimulating our appetites.

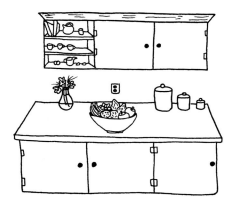

Tools of the Trade

- ❑ *Cutlery*—Your knives. We recommend a solid made 8-inch chef knife, a paring knife, a bread (serrated) knife, and a steak knife set to complete your basic kitchen cutlery needs.
- ❑ *Cutting boards*—Wooden cutting boards are preferred, as they are gentle on your knives; however, they are not dishwasher friendly. For meats, poultry, and fish keep a plastic cutting board on hand that can be placed safely in a dishwasher for

sanitizing and cleaning. Although trendy, stone cutting boards are not recommended, as they quickly dull the blades of your knives, and a dull knife is a dangerous knife.

❏ *Pots/pans*—We recommend a small and large saucepan, an 8-inch nonstick or stainless steel skillet, a deep dish or Dutch oven cast-iron pan, and a heavy sauté pan.

❏ *Storage*—If you want storage to be dishwasher- and microwave-safe, opt for glassware. If you don't mind handwashing, or only serving cold items, plasticware pieces can be used in that fashion. There are excellent bento box–style lunch boxes now available online or at popular retail stores. Our favorites are the lightweight stainless steel boxes that are easily washed in the dishwasher or BPA-free plastic boxes (hand wash and cold storage only). These are also safe to be dropped on hard surfaces. We also like plain glass storage containers with plastic lids for keeping foods fresh on the counter or in the fridge.

Did You Know?

When a nonstick pan gets scratched, it's time to toss the pan. Buy a cheap pan that you won't regret or think twice about tossing when it takes a beating. Avoid using metal or abrasive cleaners, including the dishwasher, on a nonstick pan. As easy as it is to discard directions on pots and pans, please take the time to read them. All nonstick pans that we've seen come with a warning about heating too hot or on high temperatures. Nonstick materials emit a gas when heated too high—a gas that can kill a bird within an enclosed room.[2] So, if you have a pet parrot, definitely keep nonstick pans out of your home. It's best to heat nonstick pans only to a medium heat, as no one wants their little ones breathing in these toxic gases.

Keep the heat to medium when using nonstick pans.

In addition, keep your nonstick pans scratch- and dent-free or use a metal non-coated pan like stainless steel or cast-iron for cooking.

Top 10 Food Safety Tips

Let's face it: getting foodborne illness is not for the faint of heart, but it's particularly dangerous for an infant, pregnant woman, or anyone with a compromised immune system. It's worth it to be safe when handling foods. Although our grandparents or parents did things one way, we now know what science says to keep foods safe. Follow these top 10 tips to keep your family safe.

1. Defrost all meats, poultry, or fish in a refrigerator overnight in cold water or in the microwave (using immediately if you choose this method)—no, not on the counter!

2. Cook all protein foods to the correct internal temperatures. The USDA Recommended Safe Minimum Internal Temperatures of beef, veal, and lamb (steaks and roasts) and fish to 145°F; pork and ground beef to 160°F; poultry to 165°F.

3. Keep your refrigerator below 39°F (every time you open it up, the temperature will go up, and the goal is to always keep cold foods below 40°F, so 39°F helps keep this a reality).

4. Avoid eating raw eggs. Even when tempted to take a taste of cookie dough, be sure to bake first before taking that bite.

5. Always wash your hands with warm, soapy water when handling eggs or raw meats.

6. Be sure to thoroughly wash anything that touched raw meats to avoid cross-contaminating. This includes tongs when cooking. If you use tongs to place food onto a grill or hot pan, be sure to wash before flipping over, or else raw product will contaminate the cooked surface.

7. Always reheat foods to an internal temperature of 165°F.

8. If a prepared food has been left out at room temperature for more than two hours, it's time to toss it. Keep cold foods cold and hot foods hot to avoid bacteria overgrowth.

9. Wash the surface of all fruits and vegetables before slicing through the skin. Even a cantaloupe or watermelon have things on the surface you don't want to contaminate the edible fruit with when slicing a knife through it.

10. Stay on top of food recalls.

Let's Get Planning

As dietitians and lovers of all things food, we find comfort in planning and preparing a meal. Cooking is one of the things that helps us mentally transition from a busy day to an evening with our families. It's one of our de-stressors, but we realize that cooking and getting a meal on the table isn't that way for everyone. Many times people ask us about cooking, meal planning, and sitting down to dinner. We cook almost every night, and prepping along the way with *mise en place* makes it a lot much easier.

Common Barriers to Planning Meals

❑ It can feel restrictive or rigid

❑ I may not feel like all foods can fit

❑ It's hard to be consistent

❑ People don't like what I cook

❑ I can't cook

One of the main barriers for getting families to enjoy a meal together is meal planning. We can feel like it's just too hard to make a nice meal so forget even trying. Over the years, we've worked with thousands of families to make meal planning doable, all the while getting kids involved in the process. Bringing back the family meal doesn't have to be a cooking show production, but it does require a game plan or strategy. This is how we plan and teach the families we counsel.

First, set a weekly time to get the whole family involved in a meal-planning meeting. Kids that are involved in cooking, shopping, and planning are often more adventurous eaters. Saying you'll plan and having a specific time for planning are not the same thing. We call this essential step the *plan to plan*. For example, Leslie and her family plan meals on Saturday mornings or Monday evenings, depending on their weekly schedules. We'll set up your family for success by selecting a day and time now.

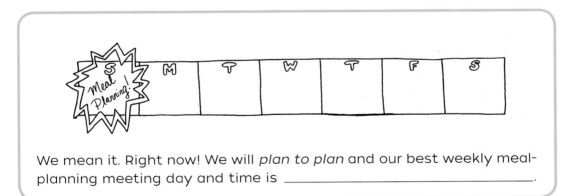

We mean it. Right now! We will *plan to plan* and our best weekly meal-planning meeting day and time is _____.

We use a meal-planning strategy, that we also mentioned in Part Two, called the Plate Method. Visualize your plate with half of the plate veggies, and the other half quarters of starchy foods and protein foods. These are the basic components of a complete meal.

1. Protein-rich foods: meats, eggs, seafood, poultry, cheese, Greek yogurt, beans, etc.

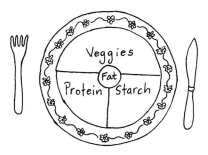

2. Vegetable/fruit side: variety is best. The different colors of vegetables mean you are getting different nutrients like dark leafy greens, peppers, Brussels sprouts, cauliflower, carrots, green beans, broccoli, berries, peaches, pears, apples, etc.

3. Starchy side: starchy veggies like peas, corn, potatoes, crackers, rice, quinoa, tortillas, breads, pasta, noodles, etc.

4. Fats: oils, nuts, avocado, butter, dressings, sour cream, etc.

Now you're ready develop your menu plan using lists of foods that you and your family like in each category. Be as specific as possible. For example, there's more than one way to serve beef, such as sirloin tips, hamburgers, flatiron steak, roast, etc. The same is true for chicken, fish, pork, etc. Get specific and don't forget to add foods you'd like to add to your menu as you're expanding your own variety. These lists gives us more options to work with meals. We'll get you started below with three different ways of serving the same main protein ingredient: chicken breast and ground beef.

Meat/Protein	Veggie/Fruit Side	Starchy Side	Satisfying Fats
Grilled Chicken Breast	Sautéed Broccoli with Parmesan	Wild Rice	Olive Oil on the Rice and Broccoli
Baked Chicken with BBQ Sauce	Baked Cauliflower with Cheddar Cheese	Baked Sweet Potatoes	Butter on the Potatoes and Olive Oil on the Baked Chicken
Slow Cooker Chicken Breast with Salsa	Lettuce, Tomato, and Salsa	Tortillas for Tacos	Sour Cream and Avocado Slices

Meat/Protein	Veggie/Fruit Side	Starchy Side	Satisfying Fats
Ground Beef in Spaghetti Sauce	Side Salad	Pasta noodles	Olive Oil in the Noodles and Salad Dressing
Cheeseburgers	Lettuce/Tomatoes and Fruit Salad	Bun	Mayo, Avocado Slices
Ground Beef in Soup	Tomatoes and Mixed Veggies in Soup	Garlic Bread	Butter on the Garlic Bread

Family Meals and Meal Planning

At your first strategy meeting, ask every eating member of your household to help you make an extensive list of ways to cook a meal component expanding beyond the type of protein or veggie. Think of foods that you've enjoyed out to eat or at a friend's house. If you have older kids or other family members, ask them to do the same. If it's just you and baby most of the time, you can make a list of foods you like and would like to try, provide for baby, or cook a new way. This can give you a good amount of options to work with later. Now, have each member of your household plan a few meals. Your extensive meal component list will help you at each meal planning meeting.

Planning meals together also helps us appreciate other preferences. Meal planning requires a little give and take that teaches us to be open to new or different foods while helping us learn to be respectful of others and their food preferences. Just remember you have to actually try a food several times before you can have a preference about that food, like Leslie and asparagus. She always jokes about taking one for the team when it's on the menu. She isn't that fond of it, although she's tried it a gazillion different ways, but she eats it because her family enjoys asparagus. If you're a part of a family, there will be plenty of preferences to consider. For example, while planning meals, Mom adds a slow-cooker pot roast to the menu. Lucy suggests chicken tenders served with tortellini for one meal while Dad adds cornbread with chili to the menu plan. Each family member contributes their ideas while the menu for the next couple of days is being planned. Here's an example:

Mom's Preferred Meal	Dad's Preferred Meal	Child's Preferred Meal
Slow Cooker Pot Roast	Chili with Ground Beef	Parmesan Chicken Tenders
Carrots, Celery, Onion	Side Salad	Green Beans
Potatoes	Cornbread	Cheese Tortellini
Butter on Potatoes	Dressing on Salad	Olive Oil on the Green Beans and Tortellini

The more you do it, the easier it gets. We promise. Like most habits, getting in a meal-planning groove takes time. And getting kids involved in food prep and cooking early on teaches them valuable life skills like understanding others' preferences while meeting their own needs and planning. Caring for oneself, and others, through the act of planning and preparing food is a crucial component of a healthy and happy independent life.

CHAPTER 12 REFERENCES

1. Amber J. Hammons and Barbara H. Fiese, "Is frequency of shared family meals related to the nutritional health of children and adolescents," *Pediatrics* 127 (6) (2011): e1565–e1574, doi: 10.1542/peds.2010-1440.https://dx.doi.org/10.1542%2Fpeds.2010-1440.

2. Katherine A Shuster, Kristie L Brock, Robert C Dysko, Victor J DiRita, Ingrid L Bergin, "Polytetrafluoroethylene Toxicosis in Recently Hatched Chickens (Gallus domesticus)," *Comparative Medicine* 62 (1) (February 2012): 49–52, Published online February 2012, PMCID: PMC3276392, date accessed August 15, 2016 https://www.ncbi.nlm.nih.gov/pmc/articles/PMC3276392/.

CHAPTER 13

THE LEARNING PLATE

> "People who love to eat are always the best people."
> —Julia Child

Leslie hated mushrooms for as long as she could remember until she was a senior in high school. She'd tried them several times during her childhood but just didn't like them. Once, while on vacation with a friend, she tried them again and liked them. Even though she didn't think she would, and was just trying to be polite, she enjoyed the flavor and texture. The mushrooms had been sautéed and had a meaty and smooth texture. From then on, Leslie looked for mushrooms cooked that way on every menu. If we're willing to keep trying, tastes and preferences can change.

For every bite we take, there's something new to learn. That learning (or creative process) is even greater for an infant, but truthfully, we never stop learning about food regardless of age. Whether it's a new color (all shades of purple are not the same), a new texture (from a mushroom to a cinnamon stick), or a new flavor (from cilantro to dark chocolate), it's easy to see how our palates evolve and how we always have the opportunity to sit down at a learning plate, adults and children alike. Every meal is an opportunity.

Colors and Textures Oh My!

We've all heard the saying that *we eat with our eyes*, and it's the truth. Color is the single most predictor of whether a person will like or dislike a meal.[1] As dietitians, who are also foodies, we think about things like carrots and sweet potatoes being the same color on the plate. We may swap the sweet potato for a roasted potato just to make sure we have variety of color on the plate as well as variety of food. Colors make a difference in meal planning and food acceptance. Do you find that your meal's colorful or monochromatic? This simple change may improve your family's overall acceptance of a meal or eating more fruits and vegetables. If just by looking at the plate, your little one decides not to try the meal, look closely at what's being served. Then search for ways to shake things up a bit.

In addition to color, most of us enjoy a variety of textures. While some textures may downright disgust our senses, others may transport our senses to a more pleasurable place. Our children are no different. Textures refer to hardness, softness, roughness, or smoothness of a food. Consider serving as many textures as you can early on to increase oral acceptance of a variety of textures later on in life.[2] Find out what textures excite or disgust your little eater and work to accommodate them while continuing to offer a variety that will challenge them. This may look like offering something slippery, something crunchy, and something smooth frequently, perhaps even in the same meal.

Puréed foods, which we do not consider solids, are all similarly textured in that they're smooth, wet, and easy to swallow. Imagine for a moment that for months, you've only eaten something smooth and then you get a plate with foods that are lumpy, crunchy, or hard. It could be confusing and shocking to the senses. Research suggests early introduction of a variety of textures influences infants' preferences later on.[3] If the texture de jour is usually smooth, there's a good chance that a texture transition or acceptance will take longer. This is important because the more flavors and foods you can introduce early on may determine a child's acceptance and willingness to try a variety of foods later on in life. Some children may take even longer to adjust to a variety of textures, leaving a parent frustrated when trying to serve more foods at home, while dining out, or advancing their little one's skills with eating and using utensils. Providing a variety of textures early on is important, which is why we feel that baby-led weaning provides a great route for a timely oral acceptance of foods in developmentally appropriate infants.[4] On the Academy of American Pediatrics Advocacy and Policy Health Initiatives official website, they also note the importance of exposing babies and children to a wide variety of flavors and textures. We understand that many babies and toddlers need to be exposed to foods multiple times before they may accept them. Remember, this can be ten, twenty, and even more exposures—don't give up. This goes for adults, too. Parents can be the greatest influence an infant or child can have. While topping a sandwich with a smiley face or cutting things into cute shapes has a place to make food fun, considering the textures and flavors of the foods plays an important role in the development of an infant's palate.

The Powerful Sense of Taste

Our sense of taste is an important predictor of foods we choose to like and dislike. We have five key taste receptors on our tongue: umami, bitter, salty, sweet, and sour. Babies are born with the ability to taste. Their sensory receptors are so sensitive that they can smell their mother instantly.[5] The only taste babies may not have at birth is for salt; it's estimated that this sense emerges at around four months of age.[6]

As we mentioned in chapter 8, zinc plays an important role in our olfactory nerve, a cranial nerve involved in our sense of smell. If a baby is deficient in zinc, he may have a blunted sense of taste and smell. You can challenge a baby's palate by serving up a juicy slice of steak with a mushroom sauce (umami—the sense that picks up meaty flavors with a velvety texture), a slice of lemon (sour) with a slice of watermelon (sweet), roasted beets or a sliced olive (which are naturally salty), and topped off with a square of dark chocolate (bitter). Voila, you have just served up a complete meal that challenges and stimulates your family's olfactories!

Beyond Yummy

Yummy. Soooo good. Tasty. Yucky. Ewwwww. Although these may be frequent descriptors we choose for foods, they lack in actually describing the complexities of the food. Now, we don't expect you to tell your eight-month-old all about the umami of the tomato sauce, but you can start talking flavor and texture early on with your toddler. Powerful descriptors can help you as a parent talk to your child about a new food. In turn, it can help your child tell you why they will or won't eat a food. These terms describing flavor and texture can empower the whole family when describing foods they both like and dislike. It can also help them to think more critically about why they like or dislike a food. This leads to food preferences over time. These are just a few examples of the many texture and flavor descriptors.

Texture	**Flavor**
Crunchy	Sugary/Sweet
Silky	Smoky
Crusty	Buttery
Crispy	Spicy
Slippery	Stale
Moist	Sharp
Tough	Earthy
Cool	Burnt
Warm	Fresh
Lumpy	Salty

Don't be discouraged if your little one displays a dislike for a food. It may also be a good idea to avoid rejoicing when they dislike the same ones you do (tempting as it may be). Your little one may pass on your favorite dish or turn up their nose to something you'd otherwise expect them to enjoy. This is part of the preference process. We've had foods we did not enjoy as kids, but can now tolerate or even like as adults (like Leslie's mushroom story). From broccoli to Brussels sprouts, people generally get over their childhood dislikes of foods the more they try to eat them. Wendy Jo despised chocolate (gasp) until she was in her twenties. She also turned her nose up at onions, peppers, Brussels sprouts, popcorn, and licorice and preferred the spaghetti noodles separate from the meat sauce on her plate. In culinary school, Wendy Jo was challenged when her taste buds were exposed to fresh Brussels sprouts, gently sautéed in olive oil with salty pancetta and finished off with a splash of fresh orange juice (yes, please). She now loves Brussels sprouts and includes them on her holiday menu.

Now, Wendy Jo is total foodie who will eat or try just about everything. She has surpassed her childhood dislikes and moved on. Interestingly, what her parents didn't stop doing was introducing these flavors to her as a child. Her mom still cooked up peppers and onions, snacked frequently on popcorn, and served up mushy Brussels sprouts. Their daughter disliking certain foods wasn't going to stop her parents from enjoying them, nor should it stop you. Serve up these foods and serve them often. Wendy Jo's palate soon got past her previous perceptions. Most of ours do!

A Story in Three Bites

There are times we may find ourselves eating for the sake of eating. Think Halloween candy or eating a snack while distracted by the television. It's hard to pinpoint the flavors or textures we like when we're not paying attention. On the flip side, we may not even realize that we're eating something we wouldn't like if we were truly giving it our attention.

One of our favorite client experiments is called the Three Bite Activity. This activity aims to teach us to slow down, tune in, and savor each bite. And, if you find you don't enjoy what you're eating, this can help us realize we don't have to continue eating the food.

The Three Bite Activity works perfectly with a piece of higher-quality dark chocolate and a piece of lower-quality chocolate candy or chocolate-coated candy. You'll either need three pieces of each or plan to take three bites of each. In this activity, focus on the *flavor, texture*, and the *overall savor-ability* of the food.

Here goes...

Bite 1: Take your piece of chocolate candy. During your first bite, focus just on *flavor*. Close your eyes and ask yourself what words you would use to describe the *flavor* of the candy.

Bite 2: Next, focus on *texture* of the chocolate candy. Is it crunchy? Is it smooth? What *textures* do you pick up?

Bite 3: Take 30 seconds to chew your last bite. Close your eyes and *savor* it all together.

Before giving your final impression, try the same process with a piece of dark chocolate.

One. Two. Three . . .

Now, think back to your overall impressions of both foods. Which satisfied you more? Why? This same principle can be applied to any food and at any meal as long as we slow down long enough to give it our full attention.

Quality Over Quantity

Throughout the years, our dieting culture has put an emphasis on numbers versus actual food quality. Say someone is counting calories and opted for a fat-free, sugar-free bowl of fill-in-the-blank food-like product because of the numbers. There's a perception that lower numbers are better. This person may have missed on a more nutritious food because they feared the higher calorie food was a lesser option. We wholeheartedly disagree and suggest that all our clients focus more on the quality of their food versus calories of that food. Don't forget that humans lived successfully without those numbers for thousands of years.

Let's take a look at a piece of your favorite type of cake—carrot, apple, pound, chocolate, or whatever it may be. If you savor a rich piece of your favorite cake, it's possible that less of it could bring you more satisfaction, especially when you tune into each bite. We've both had experiences with clients (and even personally) where we've eaten a food that may be designed to be *healthier* that removed the satisfying components of the food. We, and our clients, shortly needed to eat more and more because it just wasn't satisfying or what we consider *real*. The fats that naturally occur in foods or in recipes have a powerful purpose. Fats create a velvety and smooth mouthfeel that so many of us enjoy. The fat also provides a satisfaction that can help us signal the end of an eating experience.

The Three Bite Activity can assist *Born to Eat* parents in tuning into what they are eating, tasting, and savoring so you can teach your little one to do the same over time. This also empowers you to choose to step away from a food that really doesn't warrant that third bite. *What you chew is always up to you!* We hope we've given you some quality information to chew on so that you can make the best choice for you and your family.

Making a Plan

In chapter 11, we covered food perceptions and decisions we must make when choosing foods for our families. In chapter 12, we discussed the art of crafting a menu, and now, in chapter 13, we've covered flavor and variety on the plate. Now it's time to pull it all together. While we don't advocate for dieting or following a scripted menu plan, we understand that people like to see what meal planning looks like and have examples. Before we embark on this menu plan, promise us that you won't feel compelled to follow it to a *T* or feel guilty if you don't. This is simply our example that we'd want to share with you if you were sitting across from us in our offices. And, if you were, we'd tweak it to work for you and your family specifically. This sample menu plan is simply a way for us to provide you with ideas, show you how we add variety in our daily meals, and highlight how to include more whole foods to nourish our *Born to Eat* families.

The Learning Plate

Day/Meal	Protein-Rich Foods	Vegetable/Fruit Side	Starchy Side	Fats
Day 1				
Breakfast	Scrambled eggs	Salsa & strawberries	Toast	Butter
Snack	Cheese stick	Grapes		
Lunch	Grilled chicken (leftover from the night before perhaps)	Salad (lettuce, tomatoes, cucumbers, carrots, kidney beans, canned artichoke hearts)	Croutons	Vinaigrette (olive oil and red wine vinegar)
Snack	Peanut butter	Apple slices		
Dinner	Chicken enchiladas (pg 221)	Steamed green beans & sliced tomatoes	Tortillas (used in recipe)	Cheese (used in recipe)
Day 2				
Breakfast	Milk	Grated apple (mixed into oats)	Oatmeal	Peanut butter or chopped nuts (mixed into oats)
Snack	Boiled eggs		Pretzels	
Lunch	Tuna salad (pg 198) or leftovers	Lettuce	Low-ingredient crackers or bread	Mayo
Snack	Yogurt	Berries		
Dinner	Grilled steak	Mushroom sauce (for steak) and side salad	Baked potato	Butter & vinaigrette
Day 3				
Breakfast	Simple & Versatile Frittatas (pg 182)	Spinach (inside muffin variation) and banana		Bacon & cheese (inside muffin variation)

Day/Meal	Protein-Rich Foods	Vegetable/Fruit Side	Starchy Side	Fats
Snack			Toast	Peanut butter
Lunch	Steak (leftover)	Quinoa "pantry" salad (pg 201)	Quinoa (in salad)	Olive oil (drizzled on top of meat with tabbouleh)
Snack	Cheese stick	Watermelon slices		
Dinner	Grilled salmon (pg 175)	Lemon slices, sautéed green beans	Crusty French bread	Butter

> We frequently use foods like butter and bacon because, to us, they're delicious and satisfying additions to any meal. Our philosophy is that it's all about how your pair your foods on the plate versus singling out one particular food as good or bad. You can savor a couple slices of pizza and pair it with a side salad and a quality dressing. We do! We also love to cook up our eggs and bacon and pair it with a bowl of fresh berries. It's our belief that we can make all foods can fit; it's all about what sits with them on the rest of the plate.

It's our hope that you can use the meal-planning, pantry-stocking, and body-trust supporting tips of this part of the book to become more present and purposeful with food. When we're not overwhelmed with getting food on the table, we can have more mental energy to enjoy a well thought-out meal. We're not saying every moment or dinner has to be plugged into a spreadsheet, but in our own lives, having a plan makes meals less stressful. We're real people, too, and sometimes even we do the *shovel and run* (gasp). But most of the time, we try our best to plan and have purpose around foods and our meals.

Being less stressed can allow us to be more present with our meal and our families. It's our hope that you and your *Born to Eat* family will be able to enjoy food, each other's company, and the energy it all provides. Being present with our food and in our family time is a *Born to Eat* value that we feel has lasting benefits. Bon appétit!

CHAPTER 13 REFERENCES

1.   Charles Spence, "On the psychological impact of food colour," *Flavour* 4(21) (2015), DOI: 10.1186/s13411-015-0031-3.

2.   Dipayan Biswas, Courtney Szocs, Aradhna Krishna and Donald R. Lehmann, "Something to Chew On: The Effects of Oral Haptics on Mastication, Orosensory Perception, and Calorie Estimation," *Journal of Consumer Research* 41 (2) (August 2014): 261–273, DOI: 10.1086/675739.

3.   Gillian Harris and Helen Coulthard, "Early Eating Behaviours and Food Acceptance Revisited: Breastfeeding and Introduction of Complementary Foods as Predictive of Food Acceptance," *Current Obesity Report* 5 (2016): 113–120, Published online March 8, 2016, DOI: 10.1007/s13679-016-0202-2, PMCID: PMC4796330.

4.   Brenda Lundyl, Tiffany Field, Kirsten Carraway, Sybil Harp, Julie Malphurs, Marla Rosenstein, Martha Pelaez-Nogueras, Frances Coletta, Dana Ott, and Maria Hernandez-Reif, "Food Texture Preferences in Infants Versus Toddlers," *Early Child Development and Care* 146 (1998): 69–85, date accessed October 5, 2016, http://www2.fiu.edu/~pelaeznm/pdfs/24%20Food%20texture%20preferences.pdf.

5.   Shota Nishitani, Tsunetake Miyamura, Masato Tagawa, Muneichiro Sumi, Ryuta Takase, Hirokazu Doi, Hiroyuki Moriuchi, Kazuyuki Shinohara, "The calming effect of a maternal breast milk odor on the human newborn infant," *Neuroscience Research* 63 (1) (2009): 66–71, DOI: 10.1016/j.neures.2008.10.007.

6.   Leslie J. Stein, Beverly J. Cowart, Gary K. Beauchamp, "The development of salty taste acceptance is related to dietary experience in human infants: a prospective study," *American Journal of Clinical Nutrition* 95 (1) (January 2012): 123–129, DOI: 10.3945/ajcn.111.014282.

PART 4

THE *BORN TO EAT* KITCHEN

The number-one request we get when helping clients or friends kick off the *Born to Eat* feeding journey is to dish our favorite family recipes and how we modify these meals for a baby. We completely understand the frustration and confusion that can come with the start of the eating journey, especially if you're not comfortable in the kitchen. Throughout these final chapters, we will share our favorite first foods, quick and easy breakfasts, lunch box and snacking favorites, and our most frequently served up family dinners. Although Wendy Jo has a knack for elaborate recipe development, we both agreed that the recipes needed to be simple. Most families who have a baby on board aren't up for balancing a thirty-ingredient recipe between loads of laundry, food shopping, menu planning, changing diapers, and actually finding time to sit. We get it.

In addition to the easy recipes, we will break down what it looks like to serve a normal meal for your beginner, novice, and advanced eater. We feel this is one of the most perplexing parts of using a self-feeding approach. Look for Baby Bites, which will break down serving suggestions based on skill levels. If you need a quick refresher on skill levels, jump back to chapters 5 through 9.

So boredom doesn't strike, we've added ways to transform many of the recipes into clever carryover meals and how to shake up a basic recipe with different spices, herbs, and flavors. If you're really looking for time-saving tips, check out the freezer-friendly guides for many of our favorite meals.

> Did you know that the average family repeats the same twelve meals each year, all year long? You can shake up your favorite meals by simply changing the spices and herbs used in a recipe. Turn a basic meat loaf into a Mexican or Greek-inspired masterpiece just by shifting around the spice profile.

CHAPTER 14

OUR FAVORITE FIRST FOODS

> "The purpose of life is to live it, to taste experience to the utmost, to reach out eagerly and without fear for newer and richer experience."
>
> —Eleanor Roosevelt

Beginning the food journey was (in truth) a bit nerve-racking for Wendy Jo. Wendy Jo's husband had just returned from an overseas deployment, and they decided his return marked the perfect time to share their first meal together as a family. Based on challenging communications while he was abroad, Wendy Jo wasn't able to sufficiently prepare her husband for the self-feeding approach, and he had his concerns with veering off the traditional path of baby food. It wasn't until a couple weeks in that he began to relax and really see Miss A advance in her eating skills. Then Wendy Jo's husband was boasting to all of his friends about what a great eater Miss A was and how she could suck all the juices out of a juicy steak or devour an avocado. At the time, Wendy Jo only had the support of her two fellow dietitian friends using this approach (thanks, Leslie and

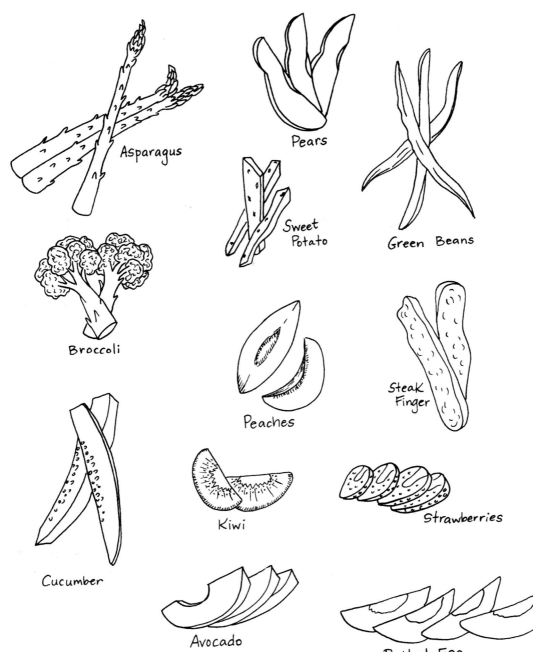

Asparagus

Pears

Sweet Potato

Green Beans

Broccoli

Peaches

Steak Finger

Cucumber

Kiwi

Strawberries

Avocado

Boiled Egg

Rebecca) and her social media channels. Unfortunately, social media doesn't always provide accurate or safe advice. There are endless questions we all face as we embark on this self-feeding journey about when to progress to solids, what food to start with, how to cook the foods, how to cut the foods, where to serve the foods, etc. The *Born to Eat* team recognized early on how important this chapter, along with chapter 5, would be for all of us embracing this approach with self-feeding babies. We hope you find these recipes and tips useful and easier than expected during those first couple weeks of supporting your self-feeding baby.

This is the exciting, yet scary, start to your baby's eating journey. As we explained back in chapter 5, every baby is different and it's important to tune into what your baby's skill and interest levels are as you progress. Even we get nervous. Miss A took a big ol' bite out of a piece of chicken early on and did gag, leaving Mom a bit unsettled. Needless to say, Wendy Jo stuck with soft veggies, steak, salmon, and chicken salad until she was ready to progress her to chicken slices at eight months. CC had a few gagging episodes, but none that were memorable. Every baby is different, and you know your little one best. Keep trying new things and go with what you feel most comfortable serving. This chapter is not about making baby foods; it's about preparing whole foods that are excellent starters for baby as well as meal components for the whole family.

This chapter includes:

Before we embark on recipes, let's take a look at higher-choking-risk foods and how they can be served safely or avoided to keep your baby safe on this self-feeding journey.

High-Choking-Risk Foods

Let's be real: a baby can choke on anything, and it's up to the parent or caregiver to make a food safe for a baby to gnaw, chew, or swallow. As we've mentioned, the BLISS study created an excellent high-risk-choking foods resource document for their study participants. We also note that study results indicated participants often served their babies high-risk foods. We felt that it was important to share ways high-risk-choking foods can be made safer for your new eater. There's no rush in giving a baby these foods, but when you decide your baby is ready, here are some tips to get you started safely.

High-Risk-Choking Foods	Modifying Risky Foods
Raw Carrots	Grate with a microplane or finest grater setting, serve mixed into moist foods, such as, yogurt, olive oil, or mashed avocado.
Raw Celery	Grate with a microplane or finest grater setting, serve mixed into moist foods, such as, yogurt, olive oil, or mashed avocado.
Raw Salad or Leaves (spinach, lettuce, arugula)	Roll up leaves, thinly slice (a.k.a. chiffonade), and sauté or cook.
Raw Apples or Hard Pears	Use a grater and serve in yogurt, oatmeal, or thin slices baked or sautéed to soften to a mash-able texture.
Rice Crackers, Potato Chips, Corn Chips	Avoid; use softer or melt-able type crackers if desired.
Whole Nuts	Avoid; however, tiny amounts of nut butters can be added to other moist foods to expose babies to nuts (e.g., yogurt, oatmeal, cooked farina). Finely minced nuts or flour can also be used (e.g.., almond meal).
Dried Fruits (raisins, cranberries, apricots, mango)	Soak in hot water for 5 minutes and chop into tiny bites.
Fresh Cherries	Use frozen and defrost, then quarter or chop up cherries.
Grapes	Avoid until a more skilled eater, then quarter (from stem top to bottom cuts, not around the equator), progress to halves (cutting from top to bottom only) as baby skill progresses.
Strawberries	Frozen, defrosted, and sliced or fresh strawberries cut into long, thin strips.
Raspberries	Frozen and defrosted or use very ripe, soft raspberries. Halve berries to serve.

Our Favorite First Foods

High-Risk-Choking Foods	Modifying Risky Foods
Blackberries	Frozen and defrosted or fresh sliced in quarters.
Cherry Tomatoes	Tomato slices are best or quarter cherry tomatoes.
Cooked Peas	Halve peas, fresh or frozen and defrosted.
Cooked Corn	Serve on the cob or cut kernels in half
Round Sausages or Hot Dogs	Avoid; or slice into rounds and then quarters.
Any hard fruit or vegetable that cannot be squished or mashed with ease using your thumb and index fingers. Tough skins can also make foods risky.	Either avoid or use the techniques mentioned above to make the fruits and vegetables a safe texture or shape for your infant. Remove skins as needed.

Boiled Eggs

Boiled eggs are a staple in our homes. Learning how to boil an egg is important whether you're making egg salad, tuna salad, deviled eggs, or just serving up boiled eggs. Sliced, boiled eggs were on our babies' plates from the start. It's a perfect protein for our little ones (and for family snacking) that delivers vitamin B_{12}, vitamin D, and many other nutrients.

Serving size: 1 finger slice (infant), 1–2 boiled eggs (adults)

Prep time: 0 minutes

Cook time: 18–22 minutes

Ingredients:

Raw eggs in shell

Directions:

1. Place eggs in a 4-quart saucepan and cover with cold water.
2. Place pan over high heat and bring to a boil. Once the water begins to boil, immediately cover and remove from heat. Set timer for 12 minutes.
3. Drain off hot water and place under cold running water for 1 minute.
4. Peel and enjoy or refrigerate for later.

Variations:

- If you want your eggs less firm, boil for 10 minutes, or for firmer eggs, set for 14 minutes.

> Older eggs, meaning eggs that have been in your refrigerator for a week or two, will peel easier, so keep an extra dozen on hand just for boiling.

BABY BITES:

Beginner	Novice	Advanced
Serve as a quartered wedge or as egg salad mashed with Greek yogurt or avocado	Serve as a whole egg and let them nibble off bites or in wedges. If a whole egg is challenging to hold, consider rolling in almond meal or slicing in half.	Chopped, whole, or in wedges

Steamed Vegetables

The question of the day (every day) is how long to steam vegetables. This table will help get you started. The times are estimated for a beginner texture. Steaming times will vary based on pots used, how quickly your burner can heat the water, and how thick cut the vegetable is. Remember to test vegetables by gently pressing between your index finger and thumb or by pressing with your tongue to the roof of your mouth. The vegetable should smash with ease for a beginner. For more advanced eaters or for parents, shave off a couple minutes.

Vegetable	Size	Steaming Time (minutes)
Asparagus	Leave whole	13–15
Beets	Whole. Peel off skin and quarter after steaming.	30–50 based on size variances; test with a fork after 30 minutes
Broccoli	2-inch stalks	12–14
Carrots	Baby carrot size	12–14
Cauliflower	2-inch florets	10–14
Green Beans	Leave whole	10–12
Green Peas	Leave whole, and halve for serving	4–6
Sweet Potatoes	Peel and cut into pinky finger–sized pieces	12–16
Zucchini	Finger-sized pieces	5–8

To steam fresh vegetables, use a steamer insert in a saucepan or put 1 inch of water in the bottom of a saucepan, bring to a simmer, cover, and steam vegetables for appropriate times. After steaming, immediately place vegetables into ice water for 1 minute to halt the cooking process and retain bright, vibrant color. Remember, pans and burners influence heat; therefore, test and make adjustments based on your kitchen needs.

If you prefer to use a microwave, be sure to test timing. Every microwave is different and wattage affects cooking time; therefore, we felt it good to mention but not list estimated times for steaming in a microwave. But generally speaking, it's takes about half the time spent steaming on the stovetop. To steam in a microwave, you can place frozen vegetables with a tablespoon of water in a bowl, cover with a microwave-safe cover, and then heat. Most microwave steaming can be done in about 5 to 8 minutes. Store-bought

Continued on page 168

frozen vegetable packages give cooking times on the packaging. Be sure to cook longer if a softer texture needs to be achieved, and always check for hot spots in food so not to burn your little one's mouth.

Serving Options:

- We don't eat naked vegetables all the time and we don't think your little one has to either. Steamed veggies taste delicious tossed with items such as olive oil, butter, lemon zest, lemon juice, fresh grated Parmesan, or fresh herbs. The sky's the limit for seasoning steamed vegetables.

Freezer Options:

- To freeze steamed veggies, cool completely, pat dry, and place in a single layer onto a baking sheet lined with parchment paper. Freeze for 4 hours then place into a freezer safe container for 1 to 3 months. To avoid freezer burn and extend freezer shelf-life, use a vacuum sealer.

Reality Bite

Most folks consider soft peaches an easy food for most infants. However, Miss A had her best gag reflex responses with cooked peaches. Needless to say, Wendy Jo opted for other fruits for the first couple months until she was ready to try peach slices again later—then Miss A rocked at chewing up the peaches with her new teeth without a gag. It pays to pay attention and not to assume all foods will be the easiest for our little ones. Before too long, they figure out the best way to chew up a food or spit it out. After all, they are *Born to Eat.*

CC's Flatiron Steak

Leslie still remembers the look on her neighbors' faces when they came in the dining room and a seven-month-old CC had a piece of steak hanging out of her fist. Once Leslie explained the self-feeding process, they said, "This makes perfect sense and can we have some of that steak?"

Hands down, this is our most popular recipe and food for new self-feeders because it delivers much-needed nutrients like iron, zinc, and protein among many others. Most of our friends and clients want to start with steak but are apprehensive because they don't know how to cook or serve it to an infant. This is an excellent recipe to start the feeding journey. If you can't find the flatiron steak cut, you can easily use this recipe with sirloin steaks.

Serving size: 1 finger slice (infant),
*   4–5 finger slices (adult)*

Makes about 5–6 adult servings

Prep time: 15 minutes + 30 minutes
*   to marinade (optional)*

Cook time: 20 minutes

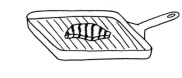

Ingredients:

2 (1-pound) flatiron steaks
2 tablespoons extra virgin olive oil

Salt and pepper to taste, or omit if
    desired

Directions:

1. Remove flatiron (or sirloin) steaks from packaging and place in a 9 × 13–inch dish.
2. Drizzle the olive oil over the steaks and evenly coat and add salt and pepper to taste.
3. Let the steaks sit at room temperature for about 30 minutes. If you are rushed to get the meal on the table you can skip this step!
4. Heat grill to 400°F (medium-high heat). You can also cook this in a skillet or grill pan at medium-high heat.
5. Grill approximately 6 to 8 minutes per side, turning only once. The thickness of the steak varies, so cook to your desired level of doneness.
6. Allow steak to rest for 5 minutes prior to slicing against the grain.

Continued on page 170

Variations:

- Dressing up a steak is easy! Top it off with sautéed mushrooms, a slice of compound butter of garlic, rosemary, salt and butter, or an extra drizzle of olive oil.

Carryover Meal Ideas:

- Top off a salad with extra slices of steak
- Chop up steak and add to a burrito or quesadilla
- Reheat or serve cold for a baby or toddler's lunch

Tip: Cut against the grain—look at the direction of the grain of the meat and then using a sharp steak knife to cut the steak at an opposing angle.

BABY BITES:

Beginner	Novice	Advanced
Sliced against the grain in a finger shape longer than baby's fist and about as wide as 1 to 2 fingers, whichever is easiest for your baby to hold.	Slice as you would for beginner and then slice in half for two smaller fingers.	Slice steak and then into bite-sized pieces.

Does your beginner baby already have teeth? If so, you could cook their steak medium-well to well done (where the meat is tough to cut through with a knife and a baby's teeth couldn't break off a piece) and serve a two finger-width piece so they don't bite off a piece just yet. The initial goal is for them to suck on the steak, gaining nutrition from the juices, and gum the meat as they learn the process of chewing.

Anya's Slow-Cooker Whole Roasted Chicken

A great way to make meat for the entire week is to cook it all at once. We love meal prepping for the week, and nothing beats plopping meat into a slow cooker, letting it cook all day, and having meat for the remainder of the week. In the beginning, Wendy Jo did a lot of slow-cooked chicken; her husband was deployed and she didn't think it was a great idea to wear the baby over a hot stove, so the slow cooker became a staple on her counter. Slow-cooking a whole chicken can actually taste like a roasted or rotisserie-cooked chicken. The trick to roasting in a slow cooker is no fluids, basting periodically, and seasoning the chicken. The veggies at the base of the dish come out a perfect texture for a beginner eater, too!

Serving size: 1 finger slice white or dark meat (infant), 3–5 oz. (adult)

Makes about 4–6 adult servings

Prep time: 15 minutes

Cook time: 6–8 hours

Ingredients:

5 carrots, scrubbed and cut into 3-inch pieces

5 celery stalks, washed and cut into 3-inch pieces

1 onion, sliced into rings

10 new potatoes, scrubbed

1 tablespoon salt (omit if desired)

1 teaspoon paprika

1 teaspoon dried thyme

1 teaspoon ground coriander

3½–4½ pound whole chicken

1 lemon

Directions:

1. Place cut vegetables in the bottom of a slow cooker.
2. Mix together spices—salt, paprika, thyme, and coriander—in a small bowl.
3. Remove the innards bag (often found in neck cavity). Rinse and pat chicken dry (be sure to clean sink after). Rub dried chicken with spice mixture, getting into all the crevices to include the inside cavity.
4. Slice lemon into quarters. Place two wedges in chicken cavity and place the other two on top of the vegetables.
5. Place chicken on top of vegetables, cover with lid, and cook on low for 8 hours or on high for 4 to 6 hours. Baste (pour pan drippings or juices over the chicken) chicken with juices every hour if possible, although not necessary.

Continued on page 172

6. Remove the chicken carefully, as it will be very tender and falling off the bone. Dark meat is tender and moist, which is great for a beginner. They can eat white or dark meat as long as it's soft and moist. Discard skin and any bones or cartilage.

Variations:

- Spice mixtures can change from Mexican (cumin, coriander, chili powder, and an orange), Greek (oregano, coriander, cumin, and olives), or Indian (curry, lime, and finely chopped cashews).

Freezer Options:

- Whatever you don't finish can be chopped and frozen to use in a variety of dishes like enchiladas, chicken salad, or chicken pot pie later.

BABY BITES:

Beginner	Novice	Advanced
A finger-like piece of dark or white meat or chopped and mashed with a little Greek yogurt, olive oil, or mayonnaise for a chicken salad. Vegetables will be very tender. Place 1 finger piece each of carrot and celery and chop up potato without skin.	Cut chicken into small, bite-sized pieces. Serve vegetables whole or chopped.	Let them enjoy a drumstick, modeling how to eat it, or chop up any part of the chicken. Serve vegetables in bite-sized pieces.

Tips:

- Add pan drippings or olive oil to the meat if it's too dry for your little one.
- Leftover chicken makes for perfect chicken salad, chicken quesadillas, chicken enchiladas, or chicken pot pie . . . or any other recipe calling for cooked chicken.

Hamburgers and Hamburger Fingers

Leslie and her family like to eat burgers. So naturally when CC was little, they made burgers and wondered how she could enjoy them too as a beginner eater. Then the hamburger finger was born.

Serving size: 1 finger patty (infant), 3–5-oz. (adult)

Makes about 4 adult servings

Prep time: 10 minutes

Cook time: 20 minutes

Ingredients:

1 pound ground beef	1 avocado, sliced
⅛ teaspoon ground black pepper	4 leaves of green lettuce
⅛ teaspoon salt, omit if desired	1 onion, thinly sliced
1 tomato, sliced	4 hamburger buns

Directions:

1. In a mixing bowl, combine ground beef with salt and pepper, as desired. Using your hands, mix lightly but thoroughly. Lightly shape into four (½-inch thick) patties and 1 to 2 beef finger-shaped pieces.

2. Place patties on grill over medium heat. Grill, over medium heat on preheated gas grill, covered, 7 to 9 minutes or until instant-read thermometer inserted horizontally into center registers 160°F, turning occasionally. If you prefer stovetop cooking, heat a dry, heavy skillet over medium-high heat. Place burgers and fingers in pan (avoid overcrowding skillet) and cover. Cook covered for 7 minutes, flip burgers, and cook for an additional 3 to 5 minutes or until a meat thermometer reads 160°F.

3. Place each burger on a bun and top with lettuce, tomato, avocado, and onion slices.

Variations (note: omit salt from infant portion if desired):

- Barbecue: mix beef with Worcestershire sauce, salt, and pepper and serve with barbecue sauce, fried onions, and pickles

Continued on page 174

- Mexican: mix beef with taco seasoning and serve with salsa, cheddar, and shredded lettuce
- Italian: mix beef with salt and pepper and serve with fresh mozzarella, tomato, and basil
- Greek: mix beef with salt, pepper, dried oregano, coriander, and crumbled feta and serve with cucumber slices, spinach, and roasted red bell peppers

Tips: If you're nervous about your baby working with a burger finger, you can try chopping and mashing with an avocado and then place pieces of this on a tray for baby. Go with your comfort level!

Baby Bites:

Beginner	Novice	Advanced
Serve a cooled hamburger finger with sliced tomato and avocado wedge all separate from one another.	Same as beginner	Make a tiny hamburger patty and serve as a mini burger or slider, just as you would enjoy it or with toppings on the side.

Grilled Salmon

Everyone raves about the importance of omega-3 fatty acids, particularly with infants. Salmon is a great source of omegas for infants. In chapter 5, we discussed safe seafood and salmon makes the list. In addition to grilled salmon, we share Wendy Jo's favorite carryover recipe for salmon patties. If you only have access to canned salmon in your area, skip right to the carryover recipe. Salmon breaks up easily and gently for beginner bites. Pair grilled salmon with steamed broccoli and mashed potatoes for a simple and complete meal.

Serving size: 2 tablespoons flaked salmon (infant), 3–5 oz. (adult)

Prep time: 10 minutes

Cook time: 16 minutes

Ingredients:

1½ pounds salmon fillets

1 lemon, zested and cut into wedges

1 tablespoon fresh dill, chopped, or
    1 teaspoon dried dill

2 cloves garlic, minced

2 tablespoons olive oil

½ teaspoon sea salt (adult portions
    only)

Directions:

1. On a baking sheet lined with parchment paper or foil, lay out salmon fillets. In a small bowl, mix together lemon zest, dill, garlic, and olive oil. Drizzle mixture evenly over salmon fillets on both sides. Season adult fillets with sea salt.
2. Heat a grill over medium-high heat.
3. Once the grill is heated to 400°F, cook fillets for 6 to 8 minutes on each side or until cooked to desired texture. Serve with lemon wedges.
4. If indoor is preferred, heat an oven to 400°F and bake salmon for 20 minutes or until desired doneness.

Variations:

- Asian-inspired with hoisin sauce and sprinkle with sesame seeds, serve with fresh lime wedges

Continued on page 176

Carryover:

- To make salmon patties: Mix together leftover cooked salmon (2 cups) with ¼ cup bread crumbs, ½ medium onion (chopped up finely), ¼ cup mayonnaise, 1 egg, a squirt of mustard, and a couple pinches of chopped fresh herbs (parsley, dill, thyme, or basil). Now, form mixture into patties and place on a baking sheet. Spray patties with olive oil spray and bake for 20 minutes. This recipe is incredible served up with plain Greek yogurt mixed with chopped garlic, lemon zest, and lemon juice. If you want to kick up the parents' version, add a squirt of sriracha sauce into the mix.

> Canned salmon can easily be mixed into scrambled eggs, served on a salad, or made into patties. Don't dismiss the goodness in the can!

BABY BITES:

Beginner	Novice	Advanced
1 to 2 tablespoons of cooked, flaked salmon or 1 finger patty of carryover recipe	3 to 4 tablespoons of cooked, flaked salmon or 1 small patty cut into bite-sized pieces of carryover recipe with sauce	¼ cup to ⅓ cup of cooked, flaked salmon or 1 small patty cut into bite-sized pieces of carryover recipe with sauce

Roasted Pork Loin with Dijon Apricot Glaze

We love a sweet and savory combo. There's no reason our little ones can't enjoy it, as well. This roasted pork loin is dressed up with apricot preserves and a little Dijon mustard. You can skip the glaze if you'd like and make it plain. It's a versatile and tasty way to cook an economical cut of meat.

Serving size: 1 finger slice (infant), 3–5 ounces (adult)

Prep time: 5 minutes

Cook time: 60 minutes

Ingredients:

1 (2–2½ pounds) pork loin roast

1 (12-oz) jar apricot or peach preserves

2 tablespoons Dijon mustard

1 tablespoon olive oil

Salt and pepper to taste, omit if desired

Directions:

1. Preheat oven to 350°F.
2. Place roast in a small roasting pan or jellyroll pan.
3. In a small bowl, mix together preserves, mustard, and olive oil. Spread half the preserves mixture on the roast and place the roast in the oven for about 60 minutes or until juices run clear, cooked to an internal temperature of 145°F to 160°F.
4. Once cooked, allow roast to cool for 10 minutes before slicing. Discard cooked sauce and juices. Use remaining uncooked sauce to drizzle over sliced pork roast. Season adult portions with salt and pepper to taste based on preference.

Variations:

This recipe also works well with applesauce instead of preserves. Unsweetened applesauce can be served to a beginner eater. It was one of CC's favorite flavor combos.

Baby Bites:

Beginner	Novice	Advanced
Serve in a pinky finger–sized slice without additional sauce.	Serve in bite-sized pieces with sauce on the side or drizzled over a couple pieces.	Serve in bite-sized pieces with sauce over top or on the side based on toddler preference.

Nutty Banana Parfaits

A great way to introduce nuts to a beginner eater is to stir nut butters into yogurt. In this recipe, we pair the sweetness of bananas with peanut butter and Greek yogurt for a delicious morning blend. We have boosted the omega-3s by tossing in chia seeds. Don't get crazy with the chia seeds—a little goes a long way. Chia seeds expand and thicken, so 1 tablespoon is plenty for this recipe.

Serving size: 2–4 tablespoons (infant), 1¼ cup (adult)

Servings: 1 adult and 1 infant

Prep time: 5 minutes

Cook time: 0 minutes

Ingredients:

1 cup whole fat, plain Greek yogurt
1–2 tablespoons peanut or almond butter
1 banana, thinly sliced
1 tablespoon chia seeds (optional)

Directions:

1. In a small mixing bowl, whisk together Greek yogurt and almond butter until well blended (about 1 minute).
2. Next, layer yogurt mixture, bananas, then chia seeds, and repeat in a serving bowl and enjoy.

Variations:

- Frozen/defrosted mangos (chopped small) + plain, unflavored coconut yogurt + cashew butter
- Chopped frozen cherries + plain Greek yogurt + almond butter
- Frozen/defrosted strawberries (chopped) + plain Greek yogurt + sunflower butter
- Add a thin layer of oats, crushed graham crackers, or minced nuts for added textures (based on skill level)

Freezer Options:

- To make a teething popsicle, pour and layer mixture into a tiny (2-ounce) cup, insert straw into center, and freeze for 4 hours or overnight before serving.

Tip: Frozen fruits are usually frozen without any sweeteners, but be sure to check the labels prior to purchasing. They make for an excellent texture for beginner eaters. If your little one is teething, gnawing on a frozen and slightly thawed piece of fruit may help ease gum discomfort.

You know your little one the best. Trust yourself to make the best and safest food decisions for your little self-feeder. If a food makes you feel uncomfortable, there's no reason to push it or question your intuition. Skip it and come back to it when you feel your little one can handle the food. Give them time to learn with safe foods, then progress as you see your self-feeder is mastering skills to move up to the next skill level of eating.

BABY BITES:

Beginner	Novice	Advanced
Serve 2 to 4 tablespoons just as you would for yourself, but consider a smock bib and something under the high chair and then let the painting—errrr, eating begin!	Serve just as described, 2 to 4 tablespoons. Smock may be helpful for easy cleanups.	Serve just as described; fruits can be in bigger pieces or chopped small.

CHAPTER 15

BREAKING THE FAST

> "The shared meal elevates eating from a mechanical process of fueling
> the body to a ritual of family and community, from the mere
> animal biology to an act of culture."
>
> —Michael Pollan, bestselling author, journalist,
> and professor at UC Berkeley

Spaghetti for breakfast anyone? For the first two months of Miss A's eating journey, Wendy Jo served up dinner for breakfast and breakfast for dinner. Miss A was a morning girl from the start who was most sharp, skilled, and ready to learn at 7:00 a.m. Knowing Miss A needed excellent iron and protein sources at breakfast, Wendy Jo often flipped the meals. Breakfast is an excellent time for beginners to eat and work on skills, because babies are often well rested, alert, and ready to learn in the mornings. Wendy Jo often opted for dinner foods for breakfast to help Miss A master her skills. Our dear friend and fellow dietitian Jane Gray found herself getting frustrated with her toddler, as he would eat everything at breakfast and lunch but struggled at dinnertime. She decided to flip her meals, too. There are no rules as to what time you eat and what foods you choose at a particular mealtime, so go with what works best for your family at whatever time that may be.

Breaking the Fast

In this chapter, we've included some of our favorite savory and (subtly) sweet breakfast dishes that are perfect at any meal but especially when breaking the fast.

This chapter includes:

We recommend omitting added sugars for those under a year old, and absolutely no honey under one year due to *Clostridium botulinum* (severe food poisoning) risks. Just a reminder: no honey means not even in baked foods. If a recipe you find calls for honey, opt for maple syrup or molasses instead.

Simple & Versatile Frittatas

Egg-based foods are an excellent way to boost vitamin D intake, protein, essential fatty acids (think brain health), and many other nutrients. In addition their great nutrition, eggs also are easy for babies to grab and hold. Eggs are considered to be a high-allergen food so parents are encouraged to introduce them early and often unless advised otherwise by your pediatrician. Egg-based pies are popular throughout the world, but in the Mediterranean, they're often referred to as frittatas. Here is a simple frittata with suggested vegetables to add based on skill. Wendy Jo and Leslie both cooked frittatas for their little ones.

Serving size: 1 finger slice (infant), ⅛ of frittata (adult)

Serves 8 adult portions

Prep time: varies based on vegetables used; basic recipe is 10 minutes

Cook time: 23 minutes

Ingredients:

Cooking spray

2 tablespoons olive oil

8 large eggs

½ cup milk or cream

¼ cup green onion, thinly sliced

1 cup fresh spinach (see notes below)

½ cup cheddar cheese, finely grated

Directions:

1. Preheat oven to 350°F. Coat 8-inch oven-safe skillet with cooking spray.
2. Heat skillet over medium with olive oil.
3. Whisk together eggs, milk, green onions, and spinach. Pour egg mixture into heated skillet and stir occasionally for 5 minutes. Stir in cheddar cheese and remove from heat.
4. Place skillet in the oven and bake for 18 minutes or until set in the center.
5. Remove from the oven, run a knife around the edge of the frittata, slightly lifting edges to help frittata loosen from pan. You can either dish it up right from the pan (Leslie's method) or remove the frittata from the skillet to serve (Wendy Jo's method). If you prefer the latter, place a plate over the top and, using two hands (and pot holders), flip frittata onto the plate. Do not remove skillet from plate. Allow frittata to rest in this position for 5 minutes before removing skillet. Slice into appropriate serving sizes based on eating skills.

Variations:

- Thinly sliced parboiled potatoes
- Quartered cherry tomatoes
- Thinly sliced zucchini slices
- Thinly sliced asparagus spears
- Fresh herbs
- Chopped smoked salmon
- Minced ham
- Crumbled bacon
- Broccoli florets

Baby Bites:

Beginner	Novice	Advanced
Chiffonade (tightly roll and thinly slice) spinach	Chop spinach	Spinach may be left whole or chopped
Serve as ½-inch to 1-inch x 3-inch finger slices of frittata (only 1 at a time to avoid overwhelming infant).	Serve as a finger or in ¼-inch bites based on infants preference and pincer grasp.	Serve in bite-sized (½-inch) pieces and encourage use of fork or spoon.
Only use vegetables you can mush with your tongue to the roof of your mouth with ease. Only use the flower portion of the broccoli florets.	Vegetables still need to be tender and in small or thinly sliced pieces (e.g., quartered cherry tomatoes, blanched and thinly sliced zucchini, blanched and chopped broccoli floret, and thinly sliced parboiled potatoes).	Vegetables still need to be tender, but raw vegetables such as zucchini, broccoli florets, and tomatoes can be used as chewing skills improve.
Parboil or steam vegetables used in frittata to help make them safe for infant to gum.		

Continued on page 184

Tips:

- When inverting a dish onto a plate, it's useful if the plate is larger than the skillet. A cutting board is also a great item to use if you do not have a plate large enough for the frittata.
- Nonstick skillets are not a good choice for baking in an oven, as they may get too hot, which is not safe for the pan. Stainless steel pans are great for frittatas.
- A pizza or pie cutter simplifies slicing of frittata.
- Frittatas may also be baked in muffin cups and frozen for later enjoyment. Freeze in airtight containers for 1 month. To reheat, wrap in damp paper towel and microwave for 30 seconds, flip, and microwave for an additional 30 seconds or until heated thoroughly (times may vary based on microwave wattage).

Cast-iron skillets heat evenly and are great moving from stovetop to oven. Be sure your cast-iron pan is well seasoned and oiled before using. If you're worried about iron or whether your baby is taking in enough iron, be sure to use a cast-iron skillet!

Leslie's Overnight Oats with Jam & Dates

These overnight oats have been a staple at Leslie's house for a few years now. Adding assorted fruit flavors with all-fruit preserves allows you to change the taste and get just the right sweetness. Overnight oats, especially when made with milk, provide satisfying protein and essential fats to get a tasty head start on your day! Enjoy this recipe with chopped dates, raisins, preserves, or any combination.

Serving size: 2 tablespoons (infant), ¼ recipe (adult)

Servings: 4 adult portions

Prep time: 5 minutes

Cook time: 0 minutes

Ingredients:

2 cups rolled oats (not instant or steel cut)

2 cups whole milk

2 teaspoons vanilla extract

½ cup dried dates or raisins, finely chopped

¼ cup 100% fruit preserves (any flavor)

Instructions:

1. In a large mixing bowl, stir the first three ingredients together. Next, stir in dates and preserves, then mix until thoroughly combined. Store in covered bowl.
2. Refrigerate bowl overnight and for up to 3 days.
3. Overnight oats can be eaten hot or cold. Leslie reheats her serving for about 30 to 60 seconds in the microwave. Test the temperature before serving to your little one.

Variations:

- Add in 1 tablespoon chia seeds
- Replace fruit jam with fresh, chopped berries, or soft cooked apples or applesauce
- Stir in 1 to 2 tablespoon nut butters to your mix

Mixes for the Win:

- Wendy Jo's favorite mix is cherry jam, sliced bananas, chia seeds, and almond butter.
- Leslie's favorite blend is applesauce and cinnamon.

Continued on page 186

Steel-cut oats aren't a good substitute for rolled oats in this recipe. Steel-cut oats are the whole oat that has been roughly chopped, whereas rolled oats have been steamed, pressed, steamed again, and toasted in their flat shape (a processed yet great food). There is little nutritional difference between the two products. Choose what works best for you and your family and the preferred texture.

Baby Bites:

Beginner	Novice	Advanced
Place 1 to 2 tablespoons on a plate for baby (try different temperatures to see which they prefer and to expose them to flavor changes that occur with heating). A loaded spoon can be introduced here, as well.	2 tablespoons to ¼ cup of oats, serve as warm, cold, or both.	¼ cup to ½ cup oats served warm or cold based on toddler's preference.

Wendy Jo's Orange Cottage Cheese Muffins

Cottage cheese is a great protein to add into a muffin recipe or pancakes. If your little one prefers pancakes, opt for cooking these up like pancakes and serve the orange marmalade as syrup, if desired.

Serving size: ¼ muffin (infant), 1–2 muffins (adult)

Prep time: 15 minutes

Cook time: 22 minutes

Ingredients:

2 cups flour

½ teaspoon baking powder

½ teaspoon baking soda

¼ teaspoon salt

¼ cup granulated sugar (omit for babies under 1 year)

1 orange, zested

1 cup whole fat small-curd cottage cheese

1 stick (½ cup) unsalted butter, softened

1 large egg

1 teaspoon vanilla extract

100% fruit orange marmalade, for the glaze

Directions:

1. Preheat oven to 350°F and line 12 muffin cups with foil liners (or paper liners gently sprayed with cooking spray to help muffins come out of wrapper).
2. In a large bowl, whisk together the flour, baking powder, baking soda, and salt.
3. In a small bowl, mix together the sugar, orange zest, cottage cheese, and softened butter.
4. Make a well in the dry ingredients and pour the wet ingredients into the well. Stir until all flour is mixed in, about 1 minute. Avoid overmixing batter.
5. Scoop ¼ cup of batter into each muffin liner or until evenly divided.
6. Bake muffins for 22 minutes or until golden on top and set in the center.
7. While muffins are baking, slightly heat orange marmalade in a microwave-safe bowl for 30 seconds.
8. Immediately after removing muffins from oven, drizzle orange glaze over the top to allow the glaze to soak into the muffins. If necessary, poke small holes in the surface of the muffins to help the syrup soak in. Serve immediately. Recommend storing leftovers in the refrigerator.

Continued on page 188

Variations:

- Add in chopped pecans or dark chocolate chips for advanced eaters.
- Dried cranberries or blueberries make great additions, too. Soak in boiling water for 5 minutes before using for beginner eaters.

Freezer Options:

- Muffins can be frozen up to 1 month in an airtight container. They can be defrosted in the refrigerator or microwave (without foil wrapper) for 20 seconds.

> Have extra ricotta on hand after making lasagna? Ricotta and cottage cheese can be used interchangeably. Yum!

BABY BITES:

Beginner	Novice	Advanced
Omit orange glaze, serve as ¼ muffin wedge	Cut muffin into small, bite-sized pieces and serve glaze on side	Cut muffin into quarters (to avoid waste) or serve them muffin as a whole with glaze

Janet's Pumpkin Bites

Pumpkin isn't just for the fall! Pumpkin is packed with vitamins, fiber, and flavor. Our fellow dietitian, friend, and *Born to Eat* mom and fan shared this recipe that she frequently whips up for her little eater.

Serving size: 2–3 bites (infant), 1 muffin (adult)

Servings: 36 bites or 12 muffins

Prep time: 10 minutes

Cook time: 8 minutes

Ingredients:

¼ cup boiling water

½ cup chopped dates

2¼ cups rolled oats

1 cup pumpkin purée

2 eggs

1 tablespoon vanilla extract

¼ cup peanut butter or almond butter

¼ cup whole milk

1 teaspoon baking powder

½ teaspoon baking soda

½ teaspoon salt

1 teaspoon cinnamon

Directions:

1. Preheat the oven to 350°F.
2. In a heat-safe bowl, pour ¼ cup boiling water over chopped dates and allow to sit for 5 minutes.
3. Line a baking sheet with parchment paper.
4. Place all the ingredients, including dates with water, into a blender or a food processor and blend for about 1 minute or until smooth.
5. Using a tablespoon, make 36 mounds on parchment paper, slightly spaced. Bake for 8 minutes or until golden brown.

Variations:

- Add in ½ cup chopped nuts or dark chocolate chips for advanced eaters. Nuts can be softened in boiling water, too, for novice eaters.
- Prefer muffins? You can bake these as muffins; simply adjust baking time to 22 minutes.

Continued on page 190

Freezer Options:

- These bites are perfect for the freezer and make for an easy, on-the-go snack later on. Once pan is cooled, place in freezer for 1 hour. Place frozen bites in a freezer-safe container and freeze up to 3 months.

Baby Bites:

Beginner	Novice	Advanced
Bake in small finger shapes for easy gripping; serve 1 to 2 bites at a time.	Serve 2 to 4 bites.	Serve 3 to 6 bites.

Egg Pancake Fingers

There is a good chance you've seen a recipe similar to this one floating around. It's easy and popular! If you're short on time, and have a ripe banana on hand, and two eggs, this is a great go-to recipe to consider. Serve these pancake fingers with whole-fat Greek yogurt mixed with a touch of nut butter for a complete meal. Fellow foodie-mama and friend Heather says her six-month-old, Teagan, didn't have a single piece left after she made these for her new self-feeder. Glad they were a big hit in her household, too!

Serving size: 1–3 finger slice (infant), 8–12 finger slices (adult)

Prep time: 5 minutes

Cook time: 10 minutes

Ingredients:

2 eggs

1 large, ripe banana

¼ cup flour, oats, or almond flour

⅛ teaspoon cinnamon

2 tablespoons coconut oil or butter

Directions:

1. In a medium mixing bowl, mash together eggs and banana for 2 to 3 minutes or until most large lumps are gone. Stir in flour of choice and cinnamon.
2. Heat a large nonstick skillet or cast-iron pan over medium heat. Add in 1 tablespoon coconut oil (or butter). Once coconut oil (or butter) is melted, make fingers of batter in the pan and cook until bubbles rise to the surface of the finger, about 3 minutes. Turn and cook until golden, approximately another minutes.
3. Melt remaining coconut oil (or butter) and cook up the rest of the batter.

BABY BITES:

Beginner	Novice	Advanced
1 to 3 pancake fingers served with 2 tablespoons of Greek yogurt mixed with 1 teaspoon of nut butter.	3 to 5 pancake fingers served with ¼ cup Greek yogurt mixed with 1 tablespoon nut butter.	Serve as you would any pancakes.

Beefy Breakfast Sausage

An excellent way to boost protein and iron in the morning is with this beefy breakfast sausage. Wendy Jo doubles the recipe and makes stuffed bread the next day or freezes to use later. Roll it up in a tortilla with scrambled eggs for a simple and complete breakfast or lunch.

Serving size: 1–2 tablespoons or 1 finger (infant), ½ cup or 1–2 patties (adult)

Serving: ~3½ cups of crumbled sausage or 8 patties

Prep time: 5 minutes

Cook time: 12 minutes

Ingredients:

1 pound ground beef	1 teaspoon cumin powder
1 teaspoon dried oregano	½ teaspoon coriander powder
1 teaspoon garlic powder	½ teaspoon salt

Directions:

1. Combine ground beef and seasonings in large bowl, mixing lightly but thoroughly.
2. To make patties or fingers, lightly shape sausage mixture into four (½-inch-thick) patties. Heat large nonstick skillet over medium until hot. Add patties; cook 10 to 12 minutes or until instant-read thermometer inserted horizontally into center registers 160°F, turning occasionally.
3. To prepare as ground sausage, heat large nonstick skillet over medium until hot. Add sausage mixture and cook 8 to 10 minutes. Break into bite-sized pieces while stirring occasionally until cooked through.

Freezer Options:

- Leftover, fully-cooked sausage can be frozen for 3 to 4 months. To use, heat large nonstick skillet over medium until hot. Add frozen crumbled sausage, and cook 6 to 9 minutes or until ground sausage reach 165°F, stirring occasionally

Baby Bites:

Beginner	Novice	Advanced
1 to 2 tablespoons of ground sausage or 1 finger patty.	2 to 4 tablespoons of ground sausage or 1 finger patty.	⅓ cup ground sausage or 2 finger patties.

CHAPTER 16

LUNCH BOX

> "One cannot think well, love well, sleep well, if one has not dined well."
> —Virginia Woolf

Let's be real here: any food can be considered lunch food. Whether it's carryovers from last night's dinner or you're craving breakfast foods at noon, all foods are a go. Bless the folks who create these adorable bento box lunches with shapes and styles—they really are adorable. To throw these ideas together, you don't need to be an artist or even crafty: simply place them in a container and call it a meal. In this chapter, we break down some of our favorite go-to lunches and family-friendly snacks. Keep it simple, sweetie! No need to stress over a lunch box. Follow this bento box guide on ways to pair up food without having to buy an overly processed cracker and lunch meat box at the grocery store. These are just as easy and much healthier!

This chapter includes:

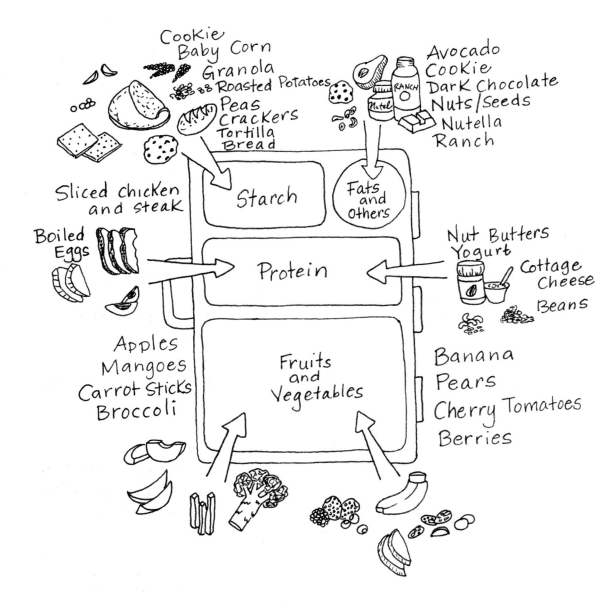

Cookie
Baby Corn
Granola
Roasted Potatoes
Peas
Crackers
Tortilla
Bread

Avocado
Cookie
Dark Chocolate
Nuts/Seeds
Nutella
Ranch

Starch

Fats
and
Others

Sliced chicken
and steak

Boiled
Eggs

Protein

Nut Butters
Yogurt
Cottage
Cheese
Beans

Apples
Mangoes
Carrot Sticks
Broccoli

Fruits
and
Vegetables

Banana
Pears
Cherry Tomatoes
Berries

CC's Avocado Chicken Salad

CC adores—no, she loves—avocados, and has since her first bite at six months of age. We all want to find ways to boost foods up with a fabulous nutrition twist, and using an avocado in place of mayonnaise is a great way to add in delicious omega fatty acids, potassium, fiber, pantothenic acid, and the list goes on. There's a reason why avocados are one of our favorite first foods for our babies. When Leslie needs a sure-thing lunch, this is her go-to chicken salad recipe. Serve the creamy chicken salad alone or with crackers, wrapped in a tortilla, as a sandwich, or just on a green salad.

Serving size: 1–2 tablespoons (infant), ½ cup (adult)

Serves: 2 adults

Prep Time: 5 minutes

Cook Time: 0 minutes

Ingredients:

- 1 cup cooked, shredded/finely chopped chicken breast, packed
- 1 ripe avocado, sliced and scored
- 2 tablespoons Greek yogurt or mayonnaise
- Salt and pepper to taste, or omit if desired

Directions:

In a medium bowl, mix all ingredients together, making sure to mash in the avocado. You can leave chunks as desired for advanced eaters.

Variation:

- Add a pinch of curry powder, grated apples, finely grated carrot, grated or minced celery, finely chopped nuts (as small as you can get them for beginner and novice eaters), or all of the above for a fancier version of curried chicken salad.

Don't Freak Out!

There's a decent amount of fat in this recipe. Fat is an important part of a healthy diet. It also helps maintain satiety to get your little one (or you) through a high-energy day.

Continued on page 196

Tips: If you have a stand mixer, you can place baked or roasted chicken breast right into the bowl with the paddle attachment on low. It will shred it right up for you! Then just toss in the rest of your ingredients. Crunched for time? You can use leftover roasted or rotisserie chicken to get this mixed up in a flash.

Baby Bites:

Beginner	Novice	Advanced
Chop up chicken finely and mix the salad (omitting salt) and serve as 1 to 2 clumps on their tray for easy grabbing.	Chop chicken finely and serve 3 to 5 spoonfuls on their tray, with soft crackers or wrapped in a tortilla (like a pinwheel sandwich).	Serve just as you would or as preferred by toddler.

Greek Yogurt Egg Salad

If your little one struggles holding on to an egg, an easy alternative is egg salad. We've given this salad a tangy boost of probiotics, calcium, and zip with Greek yogurt. This is a great first food to kick off an early introduction to both dairy and eggs.

Serving size: 1 tablespoon (infant), 1 egg (adult)

Serves 1 adult

Prep time: 5 minutes

Cook time: 0 minutes

Ingredients:

1 hard-boiled egg, peeled

1 tablespoon whole fat Greek yogurt
  (or mayonnaise)

Salt and pepper to taste, omit if desired

Directions:

1. In a small bowl, use a fork to mash up egg. Add in Greek yogurt and blend together with a couple strokes of the fork.

Variations:

• Avocados make a great swap for the yogurt and are an excellent dairy-free alternative.

Baby Bites:

Beginner	Novice	Advanced
Serve as 1 tablespoon or 3 teaspoons on their platter. A loaded spoon can be introduced here, as well.	Serve 1 to 2 tablespoons on a spoon or served with a cracker.	Serve on crackers, as a sandwich (cut into strips), or as the toddler prefers.

Chunk Light Tuna Salad

Canned chunk light tuna salad is a convenient protein product that is safe for infants. This recipe boosts the nutrition and flavors with grated carrots, onions, and Greek yogurt.

Serving size: 1–2 tablespoons (infant), ½ cup (adult)

Prep time: 5 minutes

Cook time: 0 minutes

Ingredients:

1 small carrot, finely grated
¼ small onion, finely grated
¼ cup whole fat Greek yogurt
  (or mayonnaise)

1 (6-oz) can chunk light tuna in water,
  drained
Salt and pepper to taste, omit if desired

Directions:

1. In a small mixing bowl, fork mix together finely grated carrots, onion, and Greek yogurt.
2. Next, add in the chunk light tuna and stir. Refrigerate for 1 hour before serving for the best flavor or serve immediately if you're in a rush! Season adult portion and enjoy.

> Serving a little salmon or tuna to our infants is a good thing! They can enjoy 2 to 3 age-appropriate servings per week.

BABY BITES:

Beginner	Novice	Advanced
Serve 1 to 2 tablespoons on loaded spoons or on tray for them to grab.	Serve with small spoon.	Serve rolled in a tortilla, on crackers, or as a sandwich cut into finger strips or wedges.

Wendy Jo's Dissected Salad

Salads can be easily broken down into friendly baby bites; it's all about how you plate it! Raw vegetables can be tricky, but using the smallest grater setting can add in hints of hard veggies in a safe texture (see below for our baby-friendly Cobb salad). Wendy Jo is a huge fan of raw vegetable introduction, because raw vegetables taste very different than their cooked counterparts. It's about creating a safe texture. Introducing a small amount at a time can give them exposure to the flavors that may encourage food acceptance later in life.

Serving size: see below (infant), ½ recipe (adult)

Serves: 2 adults

Prep time: 10 minutes

Cook time: 0 minutes

Ingredients:

4 cups romaine lettuce, chopped

2 hard-boiled eggs, chopped

6 cherry tomatoes, quartered

1 cup chopped meats (canned or fresh roasted chicken, canned chunk light tuna, or fresh roasted turkey)

½ avocado, chopped

1 small carrot, grated

¼ cup cheddar cheese, grated

½ cup cottage cheese

¼ cup sunflower seeds

¼ cup canned corn, drained and rinsed

½ cup canned kidney beans, drained and rinsed

⅓ cup extra virgin olive oil

¼ cup red wine vinegar

½ teaspoon dried oregano

⅛ teaspoon garlic powder

1 teaspoon prepared mustard

Salt and pepper to taste, omit if desired

Directions:

1. On a platter or two large plates, place lettuce as base for salad.
2. Next, down on the center of the lettuce, place crumbled eggs. On either side of eggs, place tomatoes, then meats, avocado, carrot, and then cheeses. Sprinkle sunflower seeds, corn, and kidney beans over the top of salads.
3. In a small bowl, whisk together olive oil, red wine vinegar, dried oregano, garlic powder, and mustard. Drizzle salads with desired dressings and season adult portions with salt.

Continued on page 200

Tips: If you see your little one gagging on a food, simply remove it from the tray once your baby releases it. Avoid reacting and continue to watch them learn and explore a variety of textures.

BABY BITES:

Beginner	Novice	Advanced
Serve salad completely dissected in little mounds: 1 tablespoon cottage cheese mixed with ½ teaspoon finely grated carrot; 1 tablespoon finely chopped meat mixed with mashed avocado; 3 mashed or halved kidney beans. Omit dressing or drizzle with olive oil only.	1 tablespoon cottage cheese mixed with 1 teaspoon finely grated carrot and sunflower seeds; 1 to 2 tomato slices with a drizzle of dressing; 1 avocado spear; 4 mashed or halved kidney beans; 1 to 2 tablespoons chopped meat.	Any combination based on toddler preferences: 1 cherry tomato, quartered or chopped; 1 avocado spear; 4 halved kidney beans; 2 to 4 tablespoons chopped meat; 1 tablespoon cottage cheese mixed with sliced corn, sunflower seeds, cheddar cheese, and finely grated carrots.

*Avoid placing too much on their plates—too much food on plates can overstimulate new eaters. Don't forget to offer seconds and even thirds if needed. Enjoy your complex salad and keep it simple for the little ones.

Quinoa "Pantry" Salad

This is one of Leslie's favorite staple recipes. It's easy to make with ample leftovers for lunches throughout the week. There's reason she calls it "pantry" salad—because anything in her pantry is fair game for being tossed into this salad. Open up your pantry and give it a try!

Serving size: 2 tablespoons (infant), ½ cup (adult)

Serves: 10–12 adult portions

Prep Time: 10 minutes

Cook Time: 15 minutes

Chill Time: 2 hours

Ingredients:

2 cups dried quinoa

4 cups chicken stock, no salt added or vegetable stock or water

1 tablespoon dried oregano

1 (3.5–4 oz.) jar roasted red peppers, drained and chopped

1 (14-oz.) can artichoke hearts, drained and chopped

¼ cup drained and rinsed capers or olives

1 (4-oz.) package feta cheese crumbles

Extra virgin olive oil, ⅓ cup (more as desired)

⅓–½ cups parsley leaves, washed, dried, and chopped fresh

Salt and fresh cracked pepper to taste (omit for babies under 1 year)

Directions:

1. Prepare quinoa as directed using stock as your liquid (instead of water to add more protein and flavor). Once cooked, place in large mixing bowl and refrigerate for at least 1 hour.

2. Once cooled, you can mix in all the tasty stuff! Feel free to leave out anything you dislike, but the olive oil is nonnegotiable. Mix preferred ingredients and chill for 1 additional hour. Enjoy for several days. Salad can be served warm or cold and topped with any protein source you have around.

Continued on page 202

Time-saver

Once this salad is prepared, you have ample options for carry-over meals. One idea could be to toss in grilled chicken or steak for an easy lunch. This salad is great warm or cold, so it's perfect for trips to the park or play groups. Miss A had a knack for tossing the little grains everywhere; therefore, Wendy Jo got smart and started mixing any small grains (like quinoa, rice, or bulgur) with hummus or mashed beans to help hold the grains together and make clean up a bit easier.

Quesadillas

If you're bored with sandwiches or dislike bread, opt for a quesadilla. This makes for a quick lunch that can pack in a lot of fun, nutritious foods. Miss A calls this her Mexican pizza when Wendy Jo tops it with fresh tomatoes. CC loves a cheese dee-ya filled with leftover meat and veggies. This is our basic, but the options are limitless.

Serving size: 1 finger slice (infant), 1 quesadilla (adult)

Serves 1 adult

Prep time: 5 minutes

Cook time: 8 minutes

Ingredients:

Cooking spray
2 small corn or flour tortillas
2 tablespoons mashed black or pinto beans or refried beans
⅓ cup grated cheddar, Monterey Jack, or Colby cheese

Directions:

1. Spray an 8- or 9-inch skillet with cooking spray.
2. Spread mashed beans on one side of a tortilla.
3. Heat the skillet over medium-high. Place the other tortilla in the skillet and cook for 1 minute on one side then flip to the other side for 30 seconds. Top with grated cheese and place other tortilla on top to make a sandwich. Flip tortilla to heat the unheated side until cheese has melted inside. If needed, turn down the heat so tortillas don't get crispy.
4. Allow quesadilla to cool and cut according to eater's skill.

Variations:

- Have cooked sweet potato or pumpkin on hand? Mash up and spread thinly onto one side the tortilla.
- Cooked ground beef or turkey can be mixed into the mashed beans or melted cheese to help boost protein and iron sources.

Continued on page 204

Tips:

- This is a great food to introduce fun dips for little ones. Start off with a guacamole, mild salsa, or bean dip.
- This is also a great way to use leftover protein sources and veggies. Just add thinly sliced meat, shredded cheese, and chopped veggies to your tortilla and heat in the microwave. Slice into triangles or finger-like strips and serve.
- Time-saver: Fold quesadilla in half with ingredients on bottom half and microwave for about 30 to 45 seconds, depending on your microwave. Let cool and slice.

Baby Bites:

Beginner	Novice	Advanced
Serve 1 pinky finger–sized slice.	Serve 1 to 2 finger slices.	Quarter quesadilla and serve 1 to 2 wedges.

Fruit Kebabs

Fruit served on a stick is just fun for little fingers to pull or nibble off. Serve this with the following Greek yogurt dip for a protein-packed snack.

Serves 4

Prep time: 5 minutes

Cook time: 0 minutes

Ingredients:

 2 cups seasonal fruit (see chart below)
 straws

Directions:

1. Wash fruits and pat dry.
2. Using hard, flexi, or stainless-steel straws (your preference) gently skewer the fruit, trying not to break up the pieces.

Tips:

- If you're struggling or worried about breaking the fruit with the straw, you can pre-poke holes using a chopstick—save them next time you order takeout!
- Check out our seasonal list of fruits in chapter 11.
- When cutting grapes for little ones, remember to cut from pole to pole, not around the equator.
- Even fruits with a rind should be washed. As you cut through the rind, the knife will contaminate the fruit unless it's washed.

Continued on page 206

Baby Bites:

Beginner	Novice	Advanced
Skip the straw kebab and stick with beginner fruits below.	Straw (easier to hold and creates a bigger hole in center to break fruit up).	Straw (continues to be best for little ones). Use a chopstick to create a hole for harder fruits.
Blueberries; strawberries; raspberries; bananas (½-inch slices); canned or frozen cherries (be sure there are no pits).	All beginner fruits + watermelon (1-inch cubes); peach wedges (½-inch slices, skins removed); plums (½-inch slices, without peel).	All beginner & novice fruits + cantaloupe (1-inch cubes); mangos (1-inch cubes); pears (½-inch slices); grapes (halved); plums (with or without peel).
Be sure fruits are ripe enough that a baby can easily gum the fruit.	Fruits should still be ripe and soft; however, your baby has more skill and knowledge on how to maneuver fruits in their mouth. At this stage, babies will spit out pieces of foods they don't want to chew.	Your skilled baby can now gum, chew, and grind up harder fruits.

Apple Cinnamon Greek Yogurt Dip

Greek yogurt not only offers great protein, but it also provides probiotics essential for a healthy gut and immune system. This recipe softens the cultured dairy tartness and adds another super ingredient: cinnamon. This dip/spread can be made ahead and kept in the refrigerator for several days. You can hand mix this but a blender can thoroughly mix in a snap.

Serve: 1–2 tablespoons (infant) or ⅔ cup (adult)

Serves 4 as a dip or 2 adult servings

Prep Time: <5 minutes

Cook Time: 0 minutes

Ingredients:

    1 cup plain Greek yogurt
    ¼ cup applesauce
    ⅛ teaspoon ground cinnamon

Directions:

1. Mix all ingredients in a small bowl thoroughly.
2. Refrigerate until ready to use. Serve with fresh fruit, pancakes, or on its own.

Time-saver:

Have four small reusable containers ready. Fill each cup evenly and pop in the refrigerator for easy-to-grab portions.

Continued on page 208

Tip: This recipe makes for a perfect popsicle. Fill up a small paper cup with yogurt mix, place a straw in the center, and freeze until solid (about 4 to 6 hours). Once frozen, peel off the outer paper cup, enjoy, or store in a freezer-safe container for up to a week. Perfect for a teething infant. There are tiny (2-ounce) paper cups, ideal for beginner eaters.

Baby Bites:

Beginner	Novice	Advanced
Perfect for all levels. Yes, this food gets messy. Load up a spoon and allow your infant to self-feed. If your baby is struggling, you can also freeze as a popsicle and let them enjoy it frozen—great for teething, too.	Appropriate for all levels.	Perfect for all levels.

Homemade Fruit Leather

If you have a day where you'll be around the house, this is a great way to use up an abundance of fresh fruits before they spoil. For children under one year, we continue to omit added sugars and instead use apples, pears, or grapes to help make a stickier fruit leather, if that is your preference. Test your fruit purée before drying to see if it's the perfect sweetness to tartness ratio or if you need to blend in something sweet to correct the balance.

Serving size: 1 finger slice (infant), 4–5 finger slices (adult)

Servings: 2 sheet pans (~12 long rolls)

Prep time: 10 minutes

Cook time: 6–8 hours

Ingredients:

3 cups strawberries

½ cup applesauce

2 teaspoons lemon or lime juice

Directions:

1. Preheat oven to the lowest heat setting (140–170°F), best with a conventional oven setting over a convection setting, as the convection oven may dry out the mixture too fast.
2. Use a silicone baking mat or parchment paper sprayed with cooking spray on a baking sheet.
3. In a blender, blend ripe strawberries (see variations below) with applesauce and lemon juice. Check for desired sweetness. Pour a thin layer onto baking pan lined with silicone or parchment paper, leaving edges free of fruit purée.
4. Bake for 6 to 8 hours or until center is no longer moist and is set.
5. Place parchment paper or plastic wrap on a cutting board. Gently, starting from the edges, lift off fruit leather and place on a fresh piece of parchment paper or plastic wrap. Using a sharp knife or pizza cutter, cut into long strips, about 6 per pan. Cut into desired serving sizes, roll up the fruit leathers, and store in an airtight container for up to 3 weeks.

Continued on page 210

Variations:

- 2 cups strawberries + 1 cup peaches + ½ cup applesauce + 2 teaspoons lemon juice
- 2 cups blackberries + 1 cup applesauce + 2 teaspoons lime juice
- 2 cups raspberries + 1½ cup pears + 2 teaspoons lemon juice

BABY BITES:

Beginner	Novice	Advanced
Avoid with beginners.	Serve 2 to 3 finger pieces.	Serve 3 to 5 finger pieces.

CHAPTER 17

FAMILY DINNERS

> "When the joy goes out of eating, nutrition suffers."
> —Ellyn Satter, MS, RDN, MSSW

If people sit and think about what their family meal looked like growing up, and not just the food, a variety of memories come flooding back. They remember slipping food to the dog, fighting with their sister at the dinner table, eating on the way to soccer practice, or the family's favorite meal. Whether we sat at the kitchen table, in the backseat of the car, in front of the television, or in front of fancy menu items we couldn't pronounce, the memory of whatever the family meal was creates a lasting impression.

The family dinner table isn't the place for food battles or stressful conversations. It's about sharing memories of the day, giving thanks for the food on the plate, and savoring one of the few precious moments of calm in a day. Wendy Jo grew up with a strict dinner regimen that involved finishing the plate (or sitting there all night until you did), setting a proper place setting, asking to be excused, using cloth napkins, using utensils correctly, and so forth. Needless to say, there are aspects of the family dinner table we choose to keep and those we choose to lose. Her fondest memories included using cloth napkins, saying grace, and hearing about the exciting things her sisters had done throughout the day, and, of course, her mom's fried chicken or spaghetti with meat sauce.

We remember what dinner was like in our families decades later. Leslie remembers sitting down at the kitchen table with her family (and dog) most nights of the week. She remembers favorite dinners of chili, spaghetti with a side salad, beef Stroganoff, and chicken pot pies. While her parents cooked a couple nights a week, there were many evenings when brinner (breakfast for dinner) or leftovers hit the table. Luckily, besides the food, one of her fondest memories include her dad's jokes. Sometimes they were so ridiculously not funny, she couldn't help but laugh.

We thought long and hard about this chapter. We wanted to come up with simple meals for busy families. This chapter is packed with easy carryover main dishes, combo meals that are freezer friendly, simple sides, and a helpful vegetable roasting guide.

This chapter includes:

Main Dishes

Rotisserie Four Ways

No formal recipe is needed with a rotisserie chicken. Just pick up a rotisserie chicken at your local market and toss these meals together. If you're not feeling like a rotisserie bird (some come "naked" with little to no seasoning), don't forget the slow-cooker roasted chicken recipe we have in chapter 14. We've got you covered.

BABY BITES:

Beginner	Novice	Advanced
Deconstruct meal by placing meat separate from grain and vegetables. Ensure vegetables are mash-able and chicken is shredded into tiny bites. Tender pasta is okay at this stage.	You can deconstruct or keep meal whole based on skill readiness. Cut items into tiny, bite-sized pieces.	Serve as you would for the whole family, and cut into bite-sized pieces.

Continued on page 214

How We Dish It	Lemon Chicken & Veggie Penne Pasta	BBQ Chicken Pizza	Chicken & Veggie Stir-Fry	Basic Chicken Noodle Soup
What You Need	¼ cup olive oil 1 medium zucchini 1 small onion 8 oz. mushrooms 8 oz. cooked penne pasta 1 lemon Parmesan, to taste Salt and pepper, to taste	½ cup BBQ sauce 2 pita breads ¼ bell peppers, sliced ¼ onion, sliced ½ cup shredded mozzarella cheese	2 teaspoons sesame oil 1 teaspoon canola oil 1 (12-oz.) bag frozen stir-fry vegetables 1 teaspoon soy sauce 2 teaspoons sesame seeds (optional) 2 cups cooked rice or quinoa	6 cups chicken stock or broth 12–16 ounce bag of mixed veggies 6 ounces small, dried pasta ½ teaspoon ground black pepper 1 tablespoon dried parsley Fresh grated Parmesan (optional)
Simple Directions	Sauté zucchini, onion, and mushrooms in olive oil. Add the juice of one lemon. Mix all ingredients together and add grated Parmesan and salt and pepper to taste.	Preheat your oven to 425°F. Chop up your chicken meat. Mix with your preferred BBQ sauce. Place on top of a tortilla or pita. Top with shredded cheese and sliced bell peppers. Pop in the oven for 8 to 10 minutes until crisp.	Heat a medium skillet with oils over high heat, then add in stir-fry vegetables and chicken, and cook for 5 to 8 minutes or until cooked through. Season with soy sauce and sesame seeds and serve over cooked rice or quinoa.	Place stock, vegetables, and pasta into a large stockpot. Bring mixture to a boil over high heat and cook until pasta is tender (see package for times). Once the pasta is ready, reduce heat to low and throw in some chicken, ground black pepper, and dried parsley. Serve with grated Parmesan cheese.

Jane Gray's Porcupine Meatballs

Our dear friend, fellow dietitian, and *Born to Eat* mama of two boys shared her sons' favorite meatball recipe, which is packed with veggies and flavor. The rice inside the meatballs makes for a fun, porcupine-like texture, and let's face it, calling a food something fun makes it more fun to eat for little ones.

Serving size: 1–2 meatballs (infant), 8–10 meatballs (adult)

Serves: 4 adult portions

Prep time: 10 minutes

Cook time: 40 minutes

Ingredients:

1 pound ground beef	2 garlic cloves, minced
½ cup leftover cooked rice (or leftover cooked quinoa)	1 egg
	2 cups tomato juice
½ small onion, finely chopped	½ teaspoon cinnamon
1 small carrot, grated	½ teaspoon coriander
1 small zucchini, grated	2 tablespoons sugar
1 teaspoon salt, or omit if desired	2 tablespoons Worcestershire sauce

Directions:

1. In a large bowl, combine the meat, rice, onion, carrot, zucchini, salt, garlic, and egg. Shape the mixture into small balls, about 1 inch wide.
2. In a deep skillet over medium-high heat, whisk together the tomato juice, cinnamon, coriander, sugar, and Worcestershire sauce.
3. Add meatballs to skillet and simmer for 30 to 40 minutes until meatballs are cooked through. Flip meatballs occasionally and braise with liquid.

Variations:

- The meatball mixture is perfect to make into meatloaf muffin cups, too! Ditch the sauce and instead make up the meat mixture, divide into 12 muffin cups, and top with a squirt of ketchup before baking. Bake for 25 minutes or until meat is cooked thoroughly, 160°F.

Continued on page 216

Freezer Options:

- These are perfect for the freezer, too! Make a batch, cool completely after cooking, and then put into a freezer-safe container for up to 2 months. To reheat, place frozen contents in a skillet, cover, and cook over medium heat until meatball temperatures reach 165°F, about 25 minutes. Add water if the sauce gets too thick.

BABY BITES:

Beginner	Novice	Advanced
Mash up a meatball with ample sauce.	Serve 2 to 3 meatballs chopped up into bite-sized pieces with sauce.	Serve 3 to 5 meatballs with sauce, cut in half or quartered.

Easy Chili

CC and Miss A both love chili! It also makes our top-10 family dinners from growing up. Chili is excellent, whether you're from the South, the North, East, or West. It's easy, and the leftovers are always delicious. It's easy because the recipe uses canned tomatoes and canned beans (Leslie opts for canned beans and Wendy Jo soaks hers—go figure). You can use whatever products you're comfortable with, conventional or organic. Serve this chili recipe with corn bread, crackers, or corn chips.

Serving size: 2–3 tablespoons (infant), ~2 cups (adult)

Serves: 12 adult portions

Prep time: 10 minutes

Cook time: 45 minutes or 6–8 hours with a slow cooker

Ingredients:

2 pounds ground beef

2–4 tablespoons chili powder, based on preference

1 tablespoon garlic powder

2 teaspoons onion powder (or ½ medium onion, chopped)

1 teaspoon cumin powder

2 (14½-oz.) cans pinto beans, drained and rinsed

2 (14½-oz.) cans kidney beans, drained and rinsed

2 (14½-oz.) cans diced tomatoes

Fun Toppings:

sour cream

shredded cheese

green onions

Directions:

1. In a large stockpot or Dutch oven, brown meat over medium-high heat until completely cooked, about 12 minutes. Once the meat is cooked through, add seasonings to meat and cook for 1 minute.

2. If you want to use the slow cooker, transfer the meat now, add remaining ingredients, and cook on low heat for 6 to 8 hours. Otherwise, just add it all in the pot.

Continued on page 218

Open all of your cans—chili beans, kidney beans, and tomatoes. Don't forget to drain and rinse beans. Dump beans and tomatoes into pot. Bring pot to a low boil over medium-high heat, then drop temperature to low and simmer for at least 45 minutes.

3. Serve chili with or without toppings.

Freezer Options:

- Chili is perfect for the freezer. Allow chili to cool completely then place into freezer-safe containers and freeze up to 3 months. Reheat mixture on the stove top until chili reheats to 165°F or in the microwave (time based on your microwave power).

Baby Bites:

Beginner	Novice	Advanced
Mash beans and cut up ground beef into tiny bites. Be sure to check tomatoes for tenderness. Help infant by loading a spoon.	Cut beans in half and cut up ground beef into small bites. Be sure to check tomatoes, too, for tenderness. Help infant by loading a spoon.	Cut beans in half and ensure ground beef is in bite-sized pieces. Serve chili with a spoon.

Single Crust Chicken Pot Pie

Comfort food at its finest. This dish was on a monthly rotation in our homes, because it's perfect for all stages of eating and absolutely delicious. Make one for dinner and one for the freezer! Here is our number-one tip for this recipe: get all of your ingredients out and measured before starting. Once you have *mise en place*, this recipe will go quickly and smoothly, and like us, you'll find yourself ready to make it again! It's possible you won't consider buying a store-bought one after you try this.

Serving size: 2–3 tablespoons (infant), 1/6 pot pie (adult)

Serves: 6 adult portions

Prep time: 10 minutes

Cook time: 1 hour

Ingredients:

1 refrigerator-ready pie crust dough

1 pound skinless boneless chicken breast

6 medium new potatoes, chopped

2 medium carrots, sliced in half lengthwise and thinly sliced into ½ moons

1 large celery stalk, chopped small

1 tablespoon chicken stock base plus 4 cups cold water or 4 cups chicken stock

¼ cup unsalted butter

¼ cup onion, chopped

¼ cup all-purpose flour

1 teaspoon salt

¼ teaspoon black pepper

½ teaspoon dried thyme

½ teaspoon garlic powder

1 cup frozen peas

⅔ cup whole milk

Directions:

1. Spray a 9-inch-deep dish pie pan or round casserole dish with cooking spray.
2. In a 4-quart stockpot, place chicken, potatoes, carrots, and celery. Pour 4 cups cold water over chicken and veggies and stir in chicken base (don't worry about dissolving, it will). Turn burner on high heat. Once mixture comes to a boil, turn down to low, cover, and simmer for 12 minutes.
3. Preheat oven to 425°F.
4. Strain chicken and vegetables, reserving 1¾ cups of the stock (this will be used in the gravy sauce). Chop chicken into bite-sized pieces.

Continued on page 220

5. Next, in a large skillet, melt butter over medium heat then sauté onion for 3 minutes. Using a whisk, add in the flour to make the roux. Let the mixture cook over medium-low heat for 3 minutes or until golden brown in color. Using reserved liquid, whisk in stock to make a gravy. Add in chopped chicken and vegetables and stir. Add in seasonings (salt, pepper, thyme, and garlic powder). Stir in frozen peas and milk. Heat mixture for 3 minutes.

6. Pour gravy into prepared dish and top with premade pie crust. Crimp the edges and cut 5 slit marks on the top as vents for the steam while baking.

7. Cover the pan with foil and bake for 15 minutes. Remove foil and continue baking for 20 minutes or until crust is golden.

Freezer Options:

-   Double this recipe and make two! One to eat now and one for the freezer. Consider using a disposable pan for the freezer pie. Once pot pie has cooled completely, cover in plastic wrap and then foil, and freeze up to 2 months. To bake, pull out of freezer and bake at 375°F for 1 hour or until internal temperature reaches 165°F. If crust gets to golden before inside is heated, simply cover with foil and continue baking.

Baby Bites:

Beginner	Novice	Advanced
Cut peas in half, chop or mash potatoes in gravy, and shred any chicken cubes. Ensure carrots and celery are tender. Place 2 to 3 tablespoons on tray. Omit crust so baby fills up on higher protein and nutrient-dense foods first.	Cut peas in half, chop potatoes in bite-sized pieces, shred chicken in gravy, and ensure carrots and celery are tender. Place ¼ cup on tray and help infant with loaded spoons. Crust or no crust, parent discretion.	Cut peas in half, chop potatoes in bite-sized pieces, and cover small chunks of chicken in gravy. Ensure carrots and celery are tender. Serve in a bowl with spoon.

Chicken Enchilada Bake

This hearty meal is creamy and delicious. Be sure to pair the enchilada bake with a hefty side of vegetables, like a tossed salad, steamed green beans, or broccoli.

Serving size: 1–2 tablespoons (infant), ⅛ of pan (adult)

Servings: 8 adult portions

Prep time: 10 minutes

Cook time: 40 minutes

Ingredients:

3 pounds boneless skinless chicken breast, cubed

2 tablespoons extra virgin olive oil

12 taco-sized corn tortillas

1 (8-oz.) package cream cheese

1 cup sour cream

4 Roma tomatoes, chopped

salt

pepper

1 tablespoon taco seasoning

1 (15½-oz.) can enchilada sauce

8 oz. cheese of choice (Colby Jack, cheddar or Monterey Jack), shredded

1 (4-oz.) can sliced black olives, drained and rinsed (optional)

½ cup fresh cilantro, chopped (optional)

Directions:

1. Preheat oven to 350°F.
2. In a large skillet, heat olive oil over medium heat. Next, add the cubed chicken and cook completely, about 8 to 10 minutes. While the chicken is cooking, spray a 9 x 13-inch dish with nonstick spray. Using a pizza cutter, cut tortillas in half and then in half again. They should be quartered. Use half the tortillas to cover the bottom of the pan. When the chicken is cooked, remove from heat and add cream cheese, sour cream, salt, pepper, chopped tomatoes, and taco seasoning into the warm skillet. Stir thoroughly until the cream cheese and sour cream have been completely mixed. Pour the chicken mixture over the tortillas. Use the remaining tortillas to layer over the chicken mixture.
3. Pour all of the enchilada sauce evenly over the top. Cover with shredded cheese then garnish with olives if desired.

Continued on page 222

4. Bake casserole uncovered for 25 to 30 minutes. Remove from oven and let it set for 5 to 10 minutes. Top casserole with fresh chopped cilantro (optional) and serve with a heaping plate of vegetables.

Variations:

• Ground beef or leftover roasted turkey can be used instead of chicken in this recipe.

Freezer Options:

• Allow casserole to cool. Cover casserole with plastic wrap and foil to avoid freezer burn. Casserole can be frozen up to 3 months. To reheat, bake casserole at 400°F for 45 to 60 minutes right out of freezer or until sauce is bubbling. Internal temperature should measure 165°F for serving.

BABY BITES:

Beginner	Novice	Advanced
Pull out chicken pieces and shred finely with a little gravy or a dollop of Greek yogurt. Serve with an avocado wedge and thin tomato slices.	Chop up casserole into tiny bites and serve with a loaded spoon. Serve with an avocado wedge and tomato slices.	Chop up casserole into small bites and serve with a spoon or fork. Serve with a side of vegetables.

Simple Shepherd's Pie

This is another one of those recipes that looks daunting by the ingredient list; however, if you *mise en place* before cooking, it comes together quickly. If you're short on time, opt for frozen, refrigerated, or dried mashed potatoes to help. If you have leftover roast beef, pork loin, or ground meat, this is a great recipe to have a carryover meal.

Serving size: 1 finger slice (infant), 1½ cups (adult)

Servings: 4 adult portions

Prep time: 10 minutes

Cook time: 55 minutes

Ingredients:

2 medium potatoes or 6 new potatoes, scrubbed

4 oz. cream cheese

¼ cup whole milk

Salt and pepper, to taste

1 tablespoon olive oil

½ medium onion, chopped small

2 medium carrots, chopped small

1 pound ground beef or lamb

1 tablespoon Worcestershire sauce

1 tablespoon tomato paste or ketchup

1 cup frozen peas

1 cup frozen cut green beans

½ teaspoon salt, or omit if desired

½ teaspoon ground black pepper

Directions:

1. Preheat oven to 400°F.
2. Cut potatoes into large chunks or leave new potatoes whole. In a large stockpot, cover potatoes with cold water and bring to a boil over high heat. Once at a boil, turn heat down to low, cover, and simmer for 12 to 14 minutes or fork tender. Drain potatoes and mash with cream cheese and milk. Season with salt and pepper to taste.
3. Next, in a Dutch oven or large skillet, heat olive oil over medium-high heat. Add in onion and carrots and sauté for 3 minutes. Add in ground meat and cook until done, about 12 minutes. Add in Worcestershire sauce, tomato paste, frozen vegetables, salt, and pepper. Cook mixture for 5 minutes over medium heat.
4. Place cooked meat into a 9x9-inch casserole dish. Top meat mixture with potato mixture evenly. Bake shepherd's pie for 25 minutes.

Continued on page 224

Variations:

- Top off the potato mixture with grated cheddar cheese for a cheesy version.
- Skip the tomato paste and Worcestershire sauce and replace with 1 cup salsa for a quick Mexican-style shepherd's pie.

Freezer Options:

- To freeze, bake in disposable bread pans or double the batch depending on your family size. No need to bake the one going into the freezer! Simply assemble, cool completely, and cover with plastic wrap before freezing. Shepherd's pie can be frozen for up to 2 months. When you are ready to bake, remove plastic wrap, heat your oven to 350°F, and bake for 1 hour or until heated thoroughly through to a 165°F internal temperature.

BABY BITES:

Beginner	Novice	Advanced
Dissect shepherd's pie into potatoes, sliced peas, mashed green beans, and saucy meat mixture. Ensure all vegetables are easy to mash.	Dissect or keep as a casserole. Ensure peas are split and green beans are in tiny, bite-sized pieces. Serve with a loaded spoon.	Split peas in half and cut vegetables into bite-sized pieces before serving with a spoon.

Simple Sides

Dipping can be fun! Adding in sauces or dressings for dipping can make trying new foods a more enjoyable experience for little ones.

Leslie's Easy-Peasy Roasted Potatoes

Potato wedges are a popular addition to many of our meals. Unlike rice, quinoa, and couscous, potatoes make very little mess. Hey, even we like to save our paper towels sometimes!

Serving size: 2 fingerling potatoes or potato wedges (infant), 4–8 fingerling potatoes (adult)

Serves: 4–6 adults

Prep time: 10 minutes

Cook time: 30 minutes

Ingredients:

1 (1½-pound) bag of small or
    fingerling potatoes
2 tablespoons olive oil

½ teaspoon crushed black pepper
1 teaspoon dried oregano
½ teaspoon salt, or omit if desired

Directions:

1. Preheat oven to 400°F.
2. Wash and dry your potatoes. Using a cutting board, slice your fingerling or small potatoes in half lengthwise. Place in a mixing bowl and add olive oil, pepper, and oregano. Toss to coat evenly and pour onto your baking sheet. Space out on the pan. Pop in the oven for 25 to 30 minutes, stirring halfway.

Continued on page 226

Variations:

- Potatoes are very versatile. You can make a variety of spice blends (Mexican—cumin, oregano, coriander; Greek—garlic powder, rosemary; Indian—curry powder) or try a low-sodium version by roasting potatoes with just olive oil and before serving toss with fresh lemon juice and the zest of a lemon.
- Want *more* variety? Sub out potatoes for carrots, rutabagas, turnips, or any hard squash.

> If the skin is tough on the potato, try peeling it to make it easier for baby to enjoy. Fingerlings have a very thin skin, whereas russet potatoes have a thicker skin.

BABY BITES:

Beginner	Novice	Advanced
Remove skin, if desired. Check the texture to ensure potato wedges smashes with ease. Serve 1 to 2 wedges at a time.	Serve 2 wedges cut into small, bite-sized pieces.	Serve 3 to 4 as wedges or chop into bite-sized pieces.

Zucchini Fries

Zucchini, cauliflower, green beans, sweet potatoes, or butternut squash make for delicious fries simply by breading the veggies and baking. Green bean and zucchini fries are mainstays at Wendy Jo's house and a favorite of Miss A's. Make this recipe with any vegetable you like. We serve them up with a tangy sauce of mayo, Greek yogurt, lime juice and, for those who like spice, a squeeze of sriracha sauce.

Serving size: 1 finger slice (infant), 4–5 finger slices (adult)

Prep time: 20 minutes

Cook time: 20–25 minutes

Ingredients:

2 –3 large zucchinis

1 cup flour

3 teaspoons salt, divided

2 large eggs, beaten

¼ cup whole milk

2 cups panko or plain bread crumbs

½ cup flour

½ teaspoon ground cumin

½ teaspoon paprika

½ teaspoon garlic powder

Olive oil cooking spray

Directions:

1. Preheat oven to 425°F. Line two baking sheets with parchment paper or foil.
2. Slice and ready your vegetables (zucchini in ½-inch slices, cauliflower sliced in ½-inch pieces or florets, green beans are done whole).
3. Get *mise en place* by readying your breading area with 1 large plate for flour and 1 teaspoon salt, 1 large bowl for the eggs, milk, and 1 teaspoon salt, and 1 large plate for the panko, flour, and seasonings to include 1 teaspoon salt.
4. Working in batches, first dredge each piece of vegetables into flour, then dunk them into the egg mixture (letting excess drip off), and last dip into the panko mixture. Transfer breaded zucchini fries to prepared baking sheet and spray them liberally with cooking spray.
5. Bake vegetables for 20 to 25 minutes or until golden and tender.

Continued on page 228

Variations:

- Add grated Parmesan cheese and serve with a marinara dipping sauce for a fun twist!

Baby Bites:

Beginner	Novice	Advanced
Consider blanching vegetables first by putting them in boiling water for 1 to 3 minutes and then immediately into an ice bath to ensure that the veggies are mash-able once baked.	Serve 1 to 3 fries, ensuring texture is tender for a bite.	Serve 1 to 3 fries.

Parmesan Roasted Cauliflower or Broccoli

Nutrition-packed cauliflower or broccoli are a perfect nibble for new eaters. This recipe has the cauliflower thinly sliced, and as it roasts it becomes tender and the flavor is balanced by the spices and Parmesan.

Serving size: 1 finger slice (infant), 4–5 finger slices (adult)

Prep time: 5 minutes

Cook time: 20 minutes

Ingredients:

1 head cauliflower or broccoli

½ cup Parmesan cheese, grated

½ teaspoon lemon pepper

½ teaspoon dried oregano or thyme

cooking spray

Salt, to taste

Directions:

1. Preheat oven to 400°F and line two baking sheets with parchment paper or foil.
2. Remove fibrous core of cauliflower or dense stalk of broccoli. Next, cut vegetables into ¼-inch slices (yes, slices). Lay vegetables onto baking sheet. Sprinkle vegetables with Parmesan cheese, lemon pepper, and dried oregano evenly. Spray vegetables evenly with cooking spray.
3. Bake for 15 to 20 minutes or until cheese becomes golden in color and vegetables are tender with slightly browned edges. Season with salt as desired and serve.

Variations:

- Out of Parmesan? Mix grated cheddar with breadcrumbs and crumble over the top. Omit lemon pepper and use thyme to season.

> Before you toss out the thick broccoli stalks, consider peeling away the thick, fibrous part to expose the tender stalk.

BABY BITES:

Beginner	Novice	Advanced
Serve 1 to 2 cauliflower slices, ensuring texture is tender enough to mash.	Serve 2 to 3 cauliflower slices.	Serve 2 to 5 cauliflower slices

Roasted Vegetable Guide

Roasting veggies are a great way to ensure tenderness and flavor. We both use roasted veggies in our weekly menus and prepare plenty for leftovers. They're great alone or added to another dish like our versatile frittata. The general rules for roasting vegetables are as follows.

1. Fully preheat and roast at 425°F.
2. Give the vegetables some space instead of overcrowding the pan.
3. Roast vegetables of similar texture together with similar cooking time like carrots and potatoes.
4. Be liberal with the oil (you can always use the oil in salads later).
5. How small or large you dice or cut up vegetables will influence the time you need to roast. Try to keep size uniform.
6. Look for toasted edges and check for tenderness to determine doneness.

Now that you have the basics, let's break down a timetable for most vegetables:

Vegetables	Cut	Roasting Time
Potatoes, sweet potatoes, carrots, beets, or hard squashes	Cut into finger-sized pieces or large cubes	25–45 minutes
Asparagus, green beans, bell peppers, or zucchini	Whole or in strips	10–20 minutes
Broccoli, cauliflower, cabbage, or Brussels sprouts	Trim or peel off fibrous stems and cut in half or quarter	15–20 minutes
Tomatoes	Cut in half or quarter	20–25 minutes
Onions	Cut into ½-inch slices or rings	30 minutes

Tips: Any time you bake or roast foods you want the food pieces to be uniform in size to ensure even cooking.

CONCLUSION

As you kick off this journey of creating a *Born to Eat* family, we hope you will frequently pull out this book as a guidebook. We hope you've found *Born to Eat* a wonderful resource that will help you and your little one for years to come. Every bite of food has the potential to nourish a *Born to Eat* baby and family. Remember the key values behind the *Born to Eat* philosophy:

1. Eat whole food as often as possible, from the developmentally-appropriate infant through adulthood
2. Honor and support self-regulation of body nourishment
3. When possible, eat as a family
4. Be present and purposeful with food
5. Support a healthy body through body confidence, trust, and gratitude

If there are moments you feel like you're struggling or are in need of added support, check out our resources page on our website: www.BornToEatBook.com. The self-feeding and baby-led feeding approaches are gaining support worldwide, so don't ever feel as though you are alone. Social media, albeit overwhelming, has fabulous support groups or pages on a variety of social media channels. We have a list on our website to get you started.

It is our hope that the *Born to Eat* philosophy has ignited a spark in you that helps foster self-regulation and body trust in your whole family. Because we are all *Born to Eat*.

ABOUT THE AUTHORS

Photo by Reminisce Photography

Leslie Schilling

Through her years as a dietitian and nutrition expert, Leslie has practiced in many settings including infant nutrition, general pediatrics, and children with special health care needs. In addition, she focuses her own private practice on counseling families, those of all ages with disordered eating issues, and professional athletes and performers. With her warm, compassionate, and entertaining personality, Leslie has been featured in Women's Health, BuzzFeed, the Huffington Post, USNews, and HGTV. She is also the co-founder of RDs for Body Confidence, a non-diet and healthy body-image initiative for registered dietitians across North America. She owns Schilling Nutrition, a private nutrition and wellness coaching business and a online dinner menu planning service. When she's not counseling, cooking, or hanging out with her family, you can find Leslie using her social media channels and speaking platforms to deliver science-based, non-diet lifestyle and wellness messages with a dash of humor.

Photo by Christa Atwood

Wendy Jo Peterson

Between military moves and following her husband's career from state to state Wendy Jo racked up a lot of time working with children and adults across the spectrum from populations with special needs to elite athletes. Although her passion in life started while working with her culinary students and nutrition clients, becoming a mama took her passion to a new level. Wendy Jo and her husband struggled with infertility for over fifteen years before Miss A became their greatest blessing. With the struggles came a passion for fueling her body and doing the best she could for her baby, and learning as much as she could about the best way to nourish her miracle baby. As a dietitian she has been trained to challenge the norm, search the science, and move forward with an evidence-based approach. With years of working with children and feeding specialists and a focus as a culinary nutritionist, she knew a self-feeding approach was the right path for her family. Wendy Jo's mantra, *an edible approach to a life worth tasting*, goes hand-in-hand with her approach and beliefs about feeding her family and working with clients. She savors every second spent helping others to slow down and savor life too. She is the coauthor of the *Mediterranean Diet Cookbook For Dummies* and *Adrenal Fatigue For Dummies*.

ACKNOWLEDGMENTS

> "Feeling gratitude and not expressing it is like wrapping a present and not giving it."
>
> —William Arthur Ward

To Jani Moore: If it weren't for you and Chris, we wouldn't even know about this amazing and incredibly logical way to feed our kids. You and Chris gave us courage to be bold and bring our voices to light.

To our editor, Nicole Frail: Thank you for answering our endless questions, giving us great feedback, and helping *Born to Eat* come to life.

To our agent, Matt Wagner, at Fresh Books, Inc.: Thank you for you for supporting us and tirelessly hunting for the right home for *Born to Eat*.

To our amazing expert reviewers who selflessly gave their time to improve our book. Gill Rapley, PhD: without you we would have never known about baby-led weaning. You are a pioneer and your reviews truly made *Born to Eat* great! To Katja Rowell, MD: Your support and revisions helped us make *Born to Eat* a great resource for all new parents. We are honored to use resources from your amazing books in *Born to Eat*. To Jacqueline Henry, SLP: You helped us see through the eyes of a different discipline and gave us great pointers to make the book easier for parents to use. Thank you all for being early reviewers of *Born to Eat*. Our editor thanks you, too!

To our publisher, Skyhorse: We are so grateful you took a chance on us. We appreciate all you've done to make *Born to Eat* what we really wanted it to be.

Acknowledgments

To our cover designer, Jenny Zemanek: You took so many random details from us to make a beautiful and happy cover that is exactly what we wanted. Thank you!

To our illustrator, Holly Kennedy: Your drawings brought our words to life, and created whimsical, loveable images to share our visions. We appreciate your time with the whole process and love that you too are a *Born to Eat* mom.

To our friends and colleagues that contributed stories, tested recipes, reviewed the manuscript, and supported our process: Rebecca Scritchfield, Janet Borland, Blair Mize, Julie Hight, Jane Gray Bledsoe, Katie Ferraro, Sidney Fry, Lindsay Stenovec, Lindsay Livingston, Kristen Cook, Heather Wosoogh, Mimi Powell, and Courtney Hansen. We love that you all added to our knowledge base, shared fears and experiences of self-feeding babies, tested recipes, and trusted us with *Born to Eat* approach. You are a powerful and strong group of moms.

To our research advisor (Leslie's brilliantly sweet husband), Brian Schilling, PhD: Your research prowess and scientific writing knowledge was tremendously helpful and so very appreciated.

To our families: You've always pushed us, loved us, and supported us even when you had no idea what we were up to. We thank you for that!

To our girls: You have changed our lives and our worlds in the most beautiful ways. You've shown us just how big our brave is.

INDEX

CONVERSION CHARTS

METRIC AND IMPERIAL CONVERSIONS

(These conversions are rounded for convenience)

Ingredient	Cups/Tablespoons/ Teaspoons	Ounces	Grams/Milliliters
Butter	1 cup/ 16 tablespoons/ 2 sticks	8 ounces	230 grams
Cheese, shredded	1 cup	4 ounces	110 grams
Cream cheese	1 tablespoon	0.5 ounce	14.5 grams
Cornstarch	1 tablespoon	0.3 ounce	8 grams
Flour, all-purpose	1 cup/1 tablespoon	4.5 ounces/0.3 ounce	125 grams/8 grams
Flour, whole wheat	1 cup	4 ounces	120 grams
Fruit, dried	1 cup	4 ounces	120 grams
Fruits or veggies, chopped	1 cup	5 to 7 ounces	145 to 200 grams
Fruits or veggies, puréed	1 cup	8.5 ounces	245 grams
Honey, maple syrup, or corn syrup	1 tablespoon	.75 ounce	20 grams
Liquids: cream, milk, water, or juice	1 cup	8 fluid ounces	240 milliliters
Oats	1 cup	5.5 ounces	150 grams
Salt	1 teaspoon	0.2 ounce	6 grams
Spices: cinnamon, cloves, ginger, or nutmeg (ground)	1 teaspoon	0.2 ounce	5 milliliters
Sugar, brown, firmly packed	1 cup	7 ounces	200 grams
Sugar, white	1 cup/1 tablespoon	7 ounces/0.5 ounce	200 grams/12.5 grams
Vanilla extract	1 teaspoon	0.2 ounce	4 grams

OVEN TEMPERATURES

Fahrenheit	Celsius	Gas Mark
225°	110°	¼
250°	120°	½
275°	140°	1
300°	150°	2
325°	160°	3
350°	180°	4
375°	190°	5
400°	200°	6
425°	220°	7
450°	230°	8

BORN TO EAT BASICS
HANDOUT

Developmental signs of feeding readiness can include:

- Independently sitting up

- Absence of tongue thrust

- Grasping items with more hand control

- Putting toys to his or her mouth

- Demonstrating an interest in table foods

Safety Checklist

- We have taken Infant CPR

- We understand the difference between a gagging infant versus a choking infant

- We are present and eating with our baby

- Baby is in a secure, upright seat during mealtime

- We have tested the temperature and texture of each food offered

- We are allowing baby to self-feed and not putting our fingers into their mouth

Check out chapters 5-9 for feeding stages, checklists, and food progressions.

Division of Responsibility

- <u>Baby Decides:</u> What & How Much

- <u>You Decide:</u> When, Where & What Is Offered

Check Your Expectations

- Be patient with every bite and every mealtime
- Adjust mealtimes to support a happy and alert baby
- New foods can take multiple trials before a baby accepts a new food, so don't give up
- There's no such thing as a perfect food, a perfect meal, or a perfect eater
- Don't worry about how much baby is eating; every child is different, so instead look for cues of hunger/fullness and let your child be the guide

Things to Avoid

- Suggesting one more bite or encouraging a child to eat more
- Foods that can pose a choking risk, such as, whole grapes, nuts, spoonfuls of nut butters, hard vegetables or fruits, or dried fruits, see pages 164-165 in book for our extensive list on choking hazards and how to create a safer bite for your baby.

Building the Baby Plate

High Iron/Protein + High Energy + Fruit/Veggies

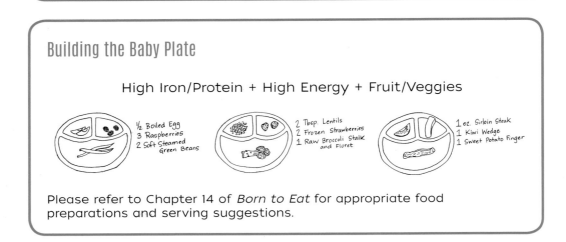

½ Boiled Egg
3 Raspberries
2 Soft Steamed Green Beans

2 Tbsp. Lentils
2 Frozen Strawberries
1 Raw Broccoli Stalk and Floret

1 oz. Sirloin Steak
1 Kiwi Wedge
1 Sweet Potato Finger

Please refer to Chapter 14 of *Born to Eat* for appropriate food preparations and serving suggestions.